Ena Baxter's
Scottish Cookbook

JOHNSTON & BACON
STIRLING

Published by
Johnston & Bacon Books Ltd.
P.O. Box No. 1,
Stirling, Scotland.

First published 1974
Reprinted 1975, 1976, 1978, 1982

ISBN 0 7179 4560 X (paperback)

Printed and bound in Great Britain by
Clark Constable Ltd., London and Edinburgh

Contents

Cover Mrs Baxter's apple and bramble pie photographed on Speyside. Recipe, see page 67.

Acknowledgements

The author and publishers would like to thank the following for their assistance.

Colour photography
The Principal of Queen Margaret College Edinburgh, who permitted the use of college facilities; and the staff and students who prepared the dishes
A. L. Hunter Photography, Edinburgh
Jenners Ltd., Edinburgh, who kindly supplied cookware and tableware
The Royal Worcester Porcelain Co. Ltd.
Josiah Wedgwood & Sons Ltd.
Hugh MacPherson (Scotland) Ltd., Highland Outfitters, Edinburgh

Cover photograph
Kindly loaned by *Gourmet* magazine, New York
Photographed by Ronny Jacques

Black and white photographs
Scottish Tourist Board
Baxters of Speyside

Map
Reiver Design, Galashiels

The author would also like to acknowledge F. Marian McNeill and Elizabeth Craig, experts in the traditional cooking of Scotland.

Foreword

I was born and brought up on a farm in Aberdeen-shire—one of the best farming and fishing counties in Scotland, and the home of the famous Aberdeen Angus cattle. Until comparatively recently it was an insular part of Scotland, isolated by the Grampian mountains and with little or no industry apart from fishing and agriculture. It was occupied by douce[1] farmers and kenspeckle[2] townsfolk who pursued their daily lives in a couthy[3] homespun fashion, changing little from one generation to the next.

My people had been farmers for many generations and consequently my brother Tom and I were brought up in the true country tradition. During my childhood, the late twenties and thirties, the farming industry was suffering from the depression and times were hard. Compared to the unemployment in the industrial cities I suppose we were fairly well off—at least we always ate well enough, though never extravagantly, and nothing was ever wasted.

The farming families were more or less self-supporting, living off what they produced on the farms—milk, oatmeal, potatoes, eggs and poultry, and also game from the hill and fish from the burn.

These basic raw materials were of excellent quality and could be made up into a variety of dishes which had been passed on from one generation to the next—never written down but learnt in the farmhouse kitchen. Some of these are the recipes which I have collected in this book, along with others which are truly traditional Scottish dishes such as powsowdie, clapshot and tattie drottle.

Despite my farming background, the life didn't appeal to me. It was my ambition to become an artist. I was teaching art in Fochabers, Moray, when I met and married Gordon Baxter, whose family business was concerned with food processing—fine quality soups, preserves, and pickles. Our first home was a small

[1] gentle. [2] colourful. [3] comfortable.

Baxter's original shop, removed from its site in Spey Street, Fochabers, and re-erected beside the modern factory, has been made into a small museum

cottage at the entrance to the factory and we both became absorbed in every activity that went on around us. It was difficult for me to adjust to this environment to begin with. Everyone talked, thought and dreamt about food and it seemed to me that it was time to practise some cooking in the quiet of my brand new kitchen. I started to browse through a magazine one day and noticed a recipe for a soup called 'Chicken Gumbo'. To me this name was so extraordinary I decided to make it to find out what it was like. It contained an unusual vegetable called okra—a green pepper found in the southern states of America—unobtainable and of course unheard of in Fochabers, so I substituted green beans from my garden. I served the soup up for supper and Gordon was so enthusiastic about it he said, 'This is a damned good soup, let's can it!' Little did I know what I had let myself in for; from then on I was in the food business.

It was easy to make a panful of soup in my own kitchen but quite a problem to put it in a can and process it. However, I persevered and eventually made it well enough to pass the most critical of tasters—my husband!

In the first year we sold 1,000,000 cans. From then on we produced a list of products including Cock-a-leekie, Pheasant Consommé, Wild Duck Consommé, Lobster Bisque, and even Minestrone!—expanding the range into exotic packs of canned pheasant, grouse and partridge in wine jellies, pâtés made from game, crab, smoked haddock and salmon, fine relishes and pickles and canned fruit—strawberries and raspberries grown on our own farms. We took the wild berries from the surrounding hills and glens and transformed them into jams and jellies.

All this activity involved travelling not only at home but around the world to find new markets for our home-made Scottish products. We met and talked to

My husband's grandmother, Margaret (top left), my mother-in-law, Ethel (top right), and myself at home at Speybank House

hundreds of people in the food business and built up relationships which today are world-wide. We gave Baxter banquets and Haggis Parties in Sydney in Australia, Chicago, Dallas in Texas, Aalborg in Denmark, Paris, and most recently in New York, in aid of the American Heart Foundation. Time never stands still and the food industry is constantly changing. It is a challenge which we strive to meet and enjoy doing so.

All this is a far cry from my mother's farmhouse kitchen. I never received any formal cookery instruction, but nevertheless I have been concerned and devoted to the art of good cooking since I became involved in the Baxter food business more than twenty years ago.

The eating and drinking habits of a nation are always interesting and the story of Scottish cooking is a fascinating piece of history; the very names of the old traditional dishes are worth preserving, and the recipes too—this is what I have tried to do by making a collection of them in this book.

Ena Baxter
March 1974

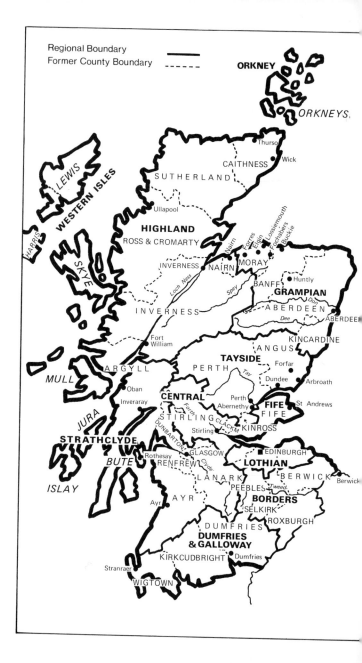

Regional Boundary ———
Former County Boundary - - - - -

ORKNEY

ORKNEYS

Thurso
CAITHNESS   Wick

S U T H E R L A N D

LEWIS

WESTERN ISLES

HARRIS

Ullapool

HIGHLAND
ROSS & CROMARTY

Forres Lossiemouth
Nairn Elgin Fochabers
Buckie
MORAY

SKYE

INVERNESS   NAIRN
Loch Ness
Huntly
Spey   **BANFF**
GRAMPIAN

I N V E R N E S S   *Don*
A B E R D E E N   ABERDEE

Dee
KINCARDINE

Fort
William

ANGUS
A R G Y L L   P E R T H   **TAYSIDE**
Forfar

MULL   Oban   *Tay*   Dundee   Arbroath

Inveraray   **CENTRAL**   Perth   **FIFE**   St Andrews
Abernethy   **FIFE**
JURA   S T I R L I N G   *Forth*   CLACKM.
DUNBARTON.   Stirling   KINROSS

STRATHCLYDE
BUTE   Rothesay   **GLASGOW**   **EDINBURGH**
ISLAY   RENFREW   *Clyde*   **LOTHIAN**

L A N A R K   PEEBLES   BERWICK   Berwick
Ayr   *Tweed.*
A Y R   **BORDERS**
SELKIRK
ROXBURGH
D U M F R I E S
DUMFRIES
& GALLOWAY
KIRKCUDBRIGHT   Dumfries
Stranraer
WIGTOWN

Soups

There has long been a great tradition of soup making and eating in Scotland. There are many reasons for this. Before people started to live in large cities it was usual for everyone to own a small garden and to grow sufficient vegetables for the household needs. It was typical of the Scottish housewife, who has always been thrifty and able to make much out of little, to make a pot of soup out of a little meat or a bone and her own vegetables, and feed a family on good nourishing fare.

A century ago in the Highlands and outer isles, where the wind and the rain make gardening very difficult, the industrious housewife would use young nettles or wild sorrel or kail to replace the cultivated varieties of vegetables so common in Scotland today.

Cock-A-Leekie

I have decided to begin this chapter with Scotland's national soup, cock-a-leekie, and one that has been popular in royal palaces and humbler dwellings in Scotland since the sixteenth century. The King (James VI and I) says in the last line of Scott's *The Fortunes of Nigel*, 'Come my lords and lieges, let us all to dinner for the cock-a-leekie is a-cooling.'

1 boiling fowl
2 quarts cold water
6 shredded leeks
1 chopped onion
2 tablespoons rice
2 teaspoons salt
good pinch of pepper
1 tablespoon chopped parsley

Draw and truss the fowl in the usual way, then place in a large saucepan with the cold water, salt and giblets. Bring slowly to the boil and skim well. Simmer gently for one hour. Add the prepared leeks, onions and the rice and continue to simmer gently until the fowl is tender. Remove the bird and the giblets and skim off any excess grease from the top of the soup. Add the parsley, taste, and season with the pepper and more salt if required. Serve the bird as the main course.

Scotch Broth

Scotch broth is the great soup of the farming families in Scotland. It is filling, nourishing and above all it is 'tasty', and a meal in itself, especially when the meat is cut in pieces and served along with the broth.

1 lb. neck of mutton or boiling beef
2 quarts cold water
1 teaspoon salt
2 tablespoons pearl barley
2 tablespoons yellow split peas
2 tablespoons dried green peas
2 medium sized carrots
2 leeks
3 tablespoons diced swede
1 medium onion
½ small cabbage
1 dessertspoon finely chopped parsley
salt and pepper to taste

Put the meat, water, salt and washed pearl barley and peas into a large saucepan. Bring to the boil very slowly, and skim. Dice the vegetables and wash and shred the cabbage and add to the pan. Bring the soup back to the boil again and simmer very gently until the meat is cooked and the peas are tender—about 2 hours. Add the parsley and salt and pepper to taste.

Partan Bree

The Scotch word for crab is 'partan' and 'bree' means liquid. This soup has been a traditional favourite with the fishing folk of Scotland for centuries.

1 large boiled crab
1 pint milk
3 oz. rice
1 pint white stock
salt and white pepper
dash of anchovy essence
$\frac{1}{4}$ pint thin cream

Remove the meat from the crab and keep aside the claw meat. Pour milk into a saucepan. Rinse the rice under cold running water in a strainer, then drain and add to the milk with a good pinch of salt. Bring to the boil. Cover with a lid and simmer until soft. Stir in the crab meat. Sieve or put into a liquidiser until smooth and creamy. Return to the pan and add the stock. Stir till boiling. Season with the salt and pepper. Add the anchovy essence and the meat taken from the claws. Stir gently until hot, but do not allow to boil. Stir in the cream and serve.

Tattie Drottle

In Scotland potatoes are called 'tatties' and they have been one of the basic ingredients in our Scottish traditional dishes for generations.

4–5 medium sized potatoes
1 leek
1 onion
salt and pepper
$\frac{1}{2}$ pint (or more) good creamy milk

Sautée chopped-up vegetables in $\frac{1}{2}$ oz. butter for a few minutes over a gentle heat. Add seasoning and $\frac{1}{2}$ pint water and cook slowly till soft. Sieve contents of the pan and add enough milk to make the consistency desired. Serve with oatcakes. This soup can be made with left-over mashed potatoes and using all milk. A sprinkling of chopped parsley improves the flavour and the appearance of this soup.

Feather Fowlie

The name of this delicious soup has always intrigued me. According to F. Marian McNeill, the Scottish food writer and historian, 'fowlie' is a corruption of 'volaille' and may be a legacy of the Auld Alliance as the soup bears a strong resemblance to 'velouté de volaille', a popular soup in France.

1 roasting fowl
2 oz. lean ham
1 sliced celery stick
1 sliced medium sized onion
2–3 carrots, sliced
2 large sprigs parsley
1 sprig thyme
1 blade mace
3 pints cold water
3 slightly beaten egg yolks
2–3 tablespoons warm cream
2 teaspoons minced parsley

Wash the fowl in salt water, then drain and joint the bird. Place joints in a basin, cover with cold salted water and soak for 30 minutes. Remove the joints and rinse under running water. Place in a large saucepan. Add the prepared vegetables, ham, herbs and mace. Pour in the cold water. Cover and bring to the boil. Skim if necessary. Simmer very slowly for $1\frac{1}{2}$ hours. Strain the stock into a basin. Allow to cool, then remove all grease.

Return the stock to a clean pan and bring very slowly to the boil. Simmer gently, uncovered, for 20 minutes. Draw the pan to side of stove. Gradually stir the egg yolks into the hot cream and then add the mixture to the soup. Add the minced parsley. Remove the breast meat from the fowl and mince it. Add to the soup as a garnish (not too much). Stir for a moment or two over a moderate heat, but do not allow to boil. 6–7 servings.

Powsowdie or Sheep's Head Broth

My mother-in-law was an expert at making this old-fashioned Scots soup and I remember well the stories she told us about her childhood when her mother sent her to the local blacksmith to get the sheep's heads well singed. This was essential to make good sheep's head broth.

1 sheep's head
1 pint vegetables cut in dice—turnip, carrot, leek
1 dessertspoon chopped parsley
2 oz. barley
1 grated carrot
3 quarts water

Have the sheep's head split in half by the butcher. Remove the brain and soak it in cold water and vinegar to blanch it. Soak the head in warm water and salt for $\frac{1}{2}$ hour. Scrape the nostril bones and cleanse the head thoroughly. Blanch the head by putting it in a pan with enough cold water to cover and bringing it to boiling point, then skimming well and pouring off the water. Put the prepared head into a large soup pot and cover it with the 3 quarts water. Add the washed barley, bring to the boil, skim, and add the diced vegetables. Season thoroughly and simmer gently for 3 to 4 hours, skimming if necessary. Add the grated carrot about $\frac{1}{4}$ hour before serving, and when the head is tender lift it out. Add the chopped parsley at the last, boil for a few minutes, then serve in a hot tureen.

Hotch potch

One of my husband's favourite soups. As soon as the new peas are ready in the garden, the family are all clamouring for hotch potch.

$1\frac{1}{2}$ lb. neck of mutton
$\frac{1}{2}$ teaspoon salt
2 quarts water
2 chopped onions
2 diced carrots
1 slice swede turnip, diced
$\frac{1}{2}$ lettuce
$\frac{1}{2}$ pint garden peas
1 medium cauliflower
1 teaspoon sugar
pepper to taste

Get the butcher to divide the meat into chops. It is very important to use fresh young vegetables as these are what give the soup so much sweet flavour. Pour the water into a large saucepan and bring to the boil. Add the meat and the salt. Boil for a minute or two then skim carefully. Cover and simmer gently for one hour. Add the prepared vegetables to stock with half the peas. Cover and bring to simmering point. Simmer for 30 minutes. Meanwhile, divide the cauliflower into small sprigs. At the end of the 30 minutes, add the cauliflower to the soup with the remaining peas. Cover and simmer till meat and vegetables are tender. Add the finely chopped parsley. Season with salt and pepper to taste. This quantity is for a large number, half the amounts given would be enough for the average family.

Partan Bree

Cock-a-leekie

Herrings in Oatmeal

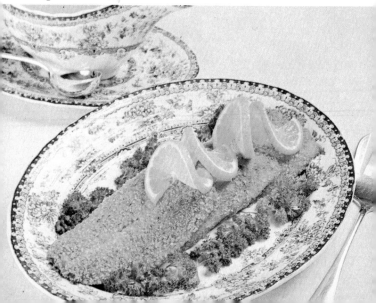

Lorraine Soup

Mary Queen of Scots has long been my favourite historical figure. This soup was probably named after her mother, Mary of Guise or Lorraine.

3 pints good white stock
1 lb. cooked, minced white meat (chicken, rabbit or veal, or a mixture)
2 oz. blanched almonds
2 hard-boiled egg yolks
1 tablespoon fine white breadcrumbs
lemon juice
¼ pint cream
1 tablespoon chopped parsley
seasonings

Mix the almonds, egg yolks and minced meat in a liquidiser. Heat the crumbs in a little stock and add to the liquidiser. Add the remainder of the stock. Season to taste with salt and pepper, powdered mace and lemon juice. Boil. Remove from the heat and stir in the cream; then reheat, but do not boil. Garnish with chopped parsley.

Tattie Soup

1 lb. boiling mutton
3 quarts cold water
2 lb. old potatoes
3 medium sized onions
1 medium sized carrot
salt and black pepper to taste
chives or parsley to garnish

Wipe the mutton with a damp cloth and place in a large saucepan. Add the water and bring to the boil. Skim carefully. Peel, slice and add the potatoes. Clean the carrot and grate. Add to the pan along with the peeled and finely chopped onions. Season with salt and pepper to taste. Cover and simmer gently for about $1\frac{1}{2}$–2 hours. Remove the mutton. Add finely chopped chives or parsley to garnish. Serves 8. This soup is a meal in itself, served with oatcakes and butter and washed down with a glass of milk.

Hough Soup

I remember arriving in Aberdeen station, one cold winter's day from London, and deciding to have a bite to eat in 'The Buffet' as it was called then. I ordered a bowl of 'soup of the day'. It was so good I asked the waitress what it was called. 'That's hough soup, lassie,' she said, 'just the very soup for a cauld day.' Here is my recipe for this old Scots soup.

1 lb. shin of beef
1 oz. beef dripping
$\frac{1}{4}$ pint sliced carrot
$2\frac{1}{2}$ pints water
1 oz. sago
$\frac{1}{4}$ pint sliced onion
2 slices turnip or swede

Wipe meat with a damp cloth. Cut into small pieces. Melt the fat in a saucepan and add the meat and prepared vegetables. Fry, turning frequently, till evenly browned and fat is absorbed. Add the water. Bring to boil and skim, then cover. Simmer gently for about $3\frac{1}{2}$ hours then skim again. Strain into a clean pan. Rinse sago in a strainer under running water then drain. Add to the soup. Bring quickly to the boil. Cover and simmer gently until sago is cooked. Season with pepper and salt to taste. Serves 4.

Fish

It has been said that herrings and oatmeal could be considered a perfectly balanced diet. They are certainly the basis of many old Scotch dishes, rich in protein and plentiful in supply.

Wha'll buy my caller herrin
They're bonnie fish and halesome farin'
New drawn frae the Forth!

Herring and Oatmeal Pie

1 lb. herrings
1 lb. potatoes
1 piece leek
2 teaspoons vinegar
1 tablespoon seasoned flour

Clean and bone herrings and cut in half. Dip in vinegar and then in seasoned flour. Roll up and put in a pie dish. Cut the leek into small pieces and slice the potatoes. Add with enough water to come half-way up the pie dish. Season the potatoes with salt and pepper.

Oatmeal Pastry

4 oz. oatmeal
4 oz. flour
$\frac{1}{2}$ teaspoon baking powder
2 oz. cooking fat
$\frac{1}{4}$ teaspoon salt

Cut the fat into small pieces and rub into the dry ingredients. Mix with cold water till it becomes a stiff paste. Roll out the pastry to the same size as the pie dish. Cover the pie with pastry and bake in a moderate oven for one hour.

Herrings fried in Oatmeal with Mustard Sauce

In my childhood our fishman called on Tuesdays and Thursdays and during the summer we had herring in oatmeal twice a week for tea. When I catch a whiff of fried herring it takes me back to long summer days in rural Aberdeenshire.

> 2 herrings per person
> oatmeal
> salt and pepper
> 1–2 oz. butter
> 1 tablespoon oil

Wash and gut the herrings. Split them and remove the back bone. Sprinkle the herrings with salt and pepper, then dip them in the oatmeal until well coated. Press the oatmeal into the flesh in order to make it stick. Meanwhile, heat the butter and oil gently. Fry the herrings, split side down, until well browned then turn and fry the other side for about 8 minutes altogether. Do not allow the pan to get too hot, otherwise the oatmeal will burn and the fish will become too dry. The oatmeal should be crisp but the flesh quite moist and succulent.

Mustard Sauce (enough for 4 herrings)

> 1 small onion or shallott
> 1 oz. butter
> 1 teaspoon dry mustard
> 1–2 tablespoons vinegar
> $\frac{1}{4}$ pint water
> $\frac{1}{2}$ oz. flour

Chop the onion finely and fry in the butter until lightly browned. Put in the flour and mustard. Add the vinegar and $\frac{1}{4}$ pint water. Bring to the boil and simmer gently for 3 minutes, stirring continuously.

Salt Herring

Around the year 1790 herring fishing became established around the Caithness coast, and with the introduction of the potato to Caithness in 1754, the staple diet for the majority of Caithness folk for the next century (and indeed it is still very popular) was tatties and herring (see next recipe). Until about twenty years ago almost every Caithness cottage had a 'firkin' of salt herring for winter use. Today they are normally supplied by the fishmonger.

The herrings are salted as follows: First remove the head and gut. Rough salt is shaken over them and the herrings are then mixed around in the salt until they are clean and shining. This process is called sousing.

The herrings are then packed in small wooden barrels (firkins). A layer of salt is placed over the bottom of the barrel then a layer of herrings packed head to tail alternately. This process continues with a layer of rough salt between each row of herrings until the barrel is full.

Tatties and Herrings

To prepare tatties and herrings for the table, remove the salt herrings from the barrel and soak in fresh water for 24 hours. Place in a saucepan of boiling water to cover and boil for 20–25 minutes, changing the water two or three times. Potatoes boiled in their jackets are the usual accompaniment. One ashet[1] of the herrings and another of potatoes are placed on the table. In olden times they were eaten with the fingers—the better to deal with the bones—so finger bowls were also provided.

Hugh Stephen, one of our factory chefs, has given me the information on the preparation of salt herring and the recipe for tatties and herrings. He is a native of Caithness and, apart from being a good chef, he is a

[1] Oval serving dish

keen sportsman and a grand musician who keeps hands
and feet tapping at our factory parties.

Salmon

Living in Moray on the banks of the River Spey, my
family are dedicated anglers. Salmon features quite often
on the menu at home, especially when we are
entertaining our overseas visitors. This is how I cook the
salmon fresh from the Spey.

Weigh the salmon, wash and drain it and put it in a fish
kettle, or a pan with a plate on the bottom, containing
boiling salted water—about one tablespoon of salt to
one quart. Simmer it gently, skimming off any scum
that may rise to the surface. Allow 8–10 minutes per
pound—plus 10 minutes extra. When the fish is cooked
it should come away easily from the bone. Remove the
fish from the pan, drain it well, take off the skin and set
the salmon aside to cool.

Sometimes vinegar is added to the water but I never
do this as I think it spoils the colour of the fish.
However, on special occasions, I add a glass of dry
white wine, which emphasises the delicate flavour of the
salmon. Never *boil* salmon, or any freshwater fish for
that matter, always *simmer*.

Best of all is to cook the salmon and other freshwater
fish in a *court-bouillon*. This is a rather overwhelming
cookery term for a simple fish stock which gives the fish
a wonderful flavour. It consists simply of 1 quart of
water and dry white wine mixed (I use 1 pint of each),
put in a pan with 1 onion, 1 clove of garlic, 1 carrot, 1
stick of celery, a bouquet garni, 1 clove, 1 tablespoon of
vinegar, 1 teaspoon of salt and some freshly ground
black pepper. Place a lid on the pan and *simmer* for at
least $\frac{1}{2}$ hour. Strain before using.

Cold Salmon Mayonnaise

¼ pint white wine
bouquet garni
1 packet aspic jelly
4½ lb. salmon
cucumber, radishes, olives etc., to garnish

Half fill a fish kettle with water, add wine and bouquet garni and bring to the boil. Carefully lower in salmon, return to the boil and simmer, allowing 10 minutes per lb. Cool fish in the water, then remove and skin. Coat with aspic (follow instructions on the packet). Garnish with radishes, cucumber, olives, hard-boiled eggs etc. Serve with mayonnaise, tossed mixed salad, vegetable salad and jacket potatoes.

Mayonnaise

2 egg yolks
½ pint olive oil } at room temperature
salt and pepper
½ teaspoon made mustard (Dijon if possible)
lemon juice or wine vinegar

Use a really clean, dry bowl and keep it steady by standing it on a tea towel wrung out in cold water. Into it put the egg yolks, salt and pepper and the mustard. Stir to a smooth paste with a wooden spoon. Blend in a few drops of lemon juice and then start adding the olive oil, very gradually, drop by drop. After the first moment or two add the oil by small teaspoonfuls otherwise it becomes very tedious. Keep stirring steadily and always in the same direction, until all the oil is absorbed. Correct the seasoning and add a little more lemon juice or vinegar to sharpen the flavour.

Salmon Trout Hollandaise

The salmon trout is very similar to the salmon in flavour and texture, but the fish itself is slightly smaller and thicker in proportion.

> 2–2½ lb. salmon trout, cleaned
> 2 fresh bay leaves
> salt and pepper
> butter

Season fish with salt and pepper and put bay leaves inside. Place on a large piece of well-buttered foil, curving fish if necessary to fit in the oven. Package foil loosely, stand on a baking sheet and cook at 400°F (Gas 6) for 30–35 minutes till tender. Leave in foil for 15 minutes. Unwrap, remove skin and place fish on a hot serving dish. Garnish with cucumber, cress and lemon wedges. Serve with the sauce, parsleyed new potatoes and fresh garden peas.

Hollandaise Sauce

> 6 tablespoons wine vinegar
> a few crushed peppercorns
> 6–8 oz. butter, softened
> 3 tablespoons water
> 4 egg yolks
> lemon juice

Boil vinegar, water and peppercorns till reduced by half. Strain into a double pan and gradually beat in the egg yolks, stirring frequently until thick. Beat in butter a little at a time until a coating consistency is obtained. Add salt, pepper and lemon juice to taste.

Serve hollandaise sauce with hot salmon and mayonnaise with cold salmon.

Here are two excellent recipes for using up left-overs—salmon kedgeree and salmon quiche. Fish cakes, too, are delicious made with left-over salmon and they are always a popular family dish.

Salmon Kedgeree

4 oz. rice
8–10 oz. cooked flaked salmon
2 oz. butter
2 finely chopped hard-boiled eggs
2–3 tablespoons cream
chopped parsley
salt, pepper and pinch cayenne pepper

Cook the rice in boiling salted water until tender, and drain well. Melt the butter in a saucepan, add the flaked salmon, the eggs, cream and seasoning and stir gently until hot. Serve the mixture in a hot dish, shape into a pyramid with a fork and serve as hot as possible. Serves 5–6.

Salmon Quiche

I am grateful to Mrs. Elizabeth Pern of the Gordon Arms Hotel in Fochabers for giving me this recipe. This cosy, friendly inn is a fishing hotel in every sense of the word, being crammed with fishermen, their wives and friends from 'a the airts' during the fishing season. The talk in the bar and at dinner is all 'fishing talk' and if anyone is lucky enough to have a big catch or to land a thirty-pounder the news is round the village in no time.

6 oz. shortcrust pastry
4 oz. cold cooked salmon
2 oz. grated cheddar cheese
$\frac{1}{2}$ oz. butter
2 eggs and 1 yolk

1 gill cream
2 oz. thinly sliced onion
salt and pepper to taste

Line a flan ring with the pastry and fill with the following mixture. Beat the eggs and the cheese together, add salt and pepper and cream. In a small saucepan, melt the butter and add sliced onions. Cook slowly until starting to colour, add the salmon and cook a little longer, stirring gently from time to time. Turn the contents of the pan into the egg mixture, mix well together and pour into the pastry case. Bake in a moderate oven until golden brown. Serve hot or cold with an accompanying salad.

Grilled Salmon Steaks

When I was first married my husband gave a small dinner party for our friends in what was then the Hydro Hotel at Forres. I chose grilled salmon steaks from a very comprehensive menu and they were superb. Needless to say they have always remained one of my favourite dishes and I serve them often at lunch parties.

2–3 slices of salmon about $\frac{3}{4}$ inch thick
salt and pepper
butter to garnish
2 tablespoons melted butter
parsley

Wipe the fish with a damp cloth and brush over with the melted butter. Season with salt and pepper. Place the slices on a well-greased grill rack and have the grill very hot. Grill each side for 6–8 minutes, according to the thickness of the slices. When done, serve on a flat dish garnished with pats of parsley butter, sprigs of fresh parsley and sliced lemon.

River Tweed

Tweed Kettle

This is a very old traditional Scottish recipe for cooking salmon and, as the name suggests, has its origins in the valley of the River Tweed and was very popular in the inns and country houses of that area in the nineteenth century.

3 lb. fresh salmon
2 shallots, very finely chopped
½ pint of water from the fish
½ pint dry white wine
pinch ground mace
2 tablespoons chopped dill or parsley
salt and freshly ground black pepper

Put the fish into a deep saucepan and cover with water. Bring slowly to the boil and simmer for five minutes. Remove the salmon from the pan, reserving the liquor. Remove the skin and bones from the fish and cut it into cubes about 2 inches square. Season with salt, pepper and mace. Put the salmon pieces back into the pan and add half a pint of the fish stock, half a pint of wine and the shallots. Cover and simmer for 25–30 minutes. Add the chopped parsley or dill before serving.

I prefer to eat Tweed kettle cold with a creamy mayonnaise or cucumber sauce.

Baked Sea Trout

The noble salmon may be reckoned to be the king among fish and prized as a great gourmet speciality, but for sheer delicacy of flavour, colour and texture, there is nothing to compare with the sea trout, or 'sea troot' as we call them on Speyside. The first fish I ever caught on the Spey was a sea trout. It was a bonnie fighter and after all the excitement had passed I carried it home in triumph and cooked it for supper.

Clean the fish and put it in a roasting tin. Pour a little *court-bouillon* (see page 18) round it and dot with butter, season with a dusting of salt and pepper. Place a few sprigs of herbs like dill, parsley or a bay leaf on the fish and cover with foil. Bake at 400°F (Gas 6) for 25–30 minutes according to size. Serve with melted butter, new potatoes and garden peas and you have a meal fit for the gods!

Lossiemouth Scampi Mornay

This is a delicious method of cooking scampi for a main course dish. It is perfect for a special lunch or for Sunday night supper.

3 oz. butter
1 lb. scampi, fresh or frozen
1½ lb. hot creamed potatoes
¼ pint milk
salt and pepper
4 oz. finely grated cheddar cheese
2 tomatoes
4 oz. button mushrooms, sliced
little seasoned flour
1¼ oz. flour
¼ pint cream
½ level teaspoon made mustard
1 tablespoon fresh breadcrumbs

Melt 2 oz. butter in a pan and sauté mushrooms for 2–3 minutes. Drain and dry scampi on absorbent paper. Toss in seasoned flour, shake off excess flour and add to mushrooms. Sauté gently for 5 minutes, stirring frequently. Pipe or spread potato round the edge of a shallow fireproof dish. Place under a hot grill until just brown. Spoon scampi and mushrooms into the centre and keep warm. Melt 1 oz. butter in a pan, stir in flour

Lossiemouth Harbour

and cook for one minute. Slowly stir in milk, bring to the boil and simmer for two minutes. Add cream, seasonings and mustard and reheat without boiling. Take off heat, stir in 3 oz. cheese and pour over scampi. Sprinkle with remaining cheese and breadcrumbs and brown under the grill. Garnish with tomatoes and serve with broccoli spears.

Creamed Haddock

This is a very tasty fish dish and makes a pleasant change from fried haddock.

> 1 lb. haddock fillets
> 4 oz. sliced mushrooms
> $\frac{3}{4}$ pint white sauce
> 2 tomatoes, sliced
> 2 tablespoons grated cheese
> 1 oz. butter or margarine

Lay the fish fillets in a fireproof dish. Cover with the sliced mushrooms and pour over the white sauce. Arrange the sliced tomatoes over the top and sprinkle evenly with grated cheese. Dot with butter or margarine. Bake in moderate oven—375°F (Gas 5)—for about 20 minutes until brown on top.

Smoked Haddock Scramble (snack or high tea)

> 1 lb. smoked haddock
> 8 eggs
> salt and pepper
> 2 oz. butter
> 2 tablespoons milk
> 1 teaspoon Worcester sauce
> 8 slices toast and butter

Poach the smoked haddock in milk for 15–20 minutes. Drain and flake. Beat the eggs together and season well. Melt the butter in a saucepan, add the milk and beaten eggs and cook over a low heat until the eggs are scrambled. Stir in the cooked flaked fish and the Worcester sauce. Check seasoning and serve on buttered toast. If desired the fish may be served whole and the eggs scrambled as an accompaniment.

Fisherman's Breakfast

My husband and my eldest son, Andrew, are enthusiastic fishermen and get up in the early morning to try to catch the elusive salmon. Needless to say, they come home ravenous. On to the stove goes the frying pan and they literally fry up everything they can find in the larder. Here is a slightly toned-down version. Serves one:

> 4–6 oz. smoked haddock fillet
> 2 rashers bacon

1 egg
1—2 oz. butter
½ oz. cooking fat
salt and pepper

Wipe the fish, dot with butter and cook in the base of grill pan under medium heat until cooked through. Baste with butter whilst cooking to keep haddock moist. Trim rind from bacon rashers and place on grill pan rack. Cook on both sides until crisp. Melt fat in frying pan and drop in egg. Sprinkle with salt and pepper. Fry until cooked and serve on a warm plate with the haddock and bacon. Garnish with fried bread and parsley.

Baked Fish Pudding

As a child I never really liked fish unless it was baked fish pudding. These were of course pre-fish finger days but I still make this fish pudding for my own family and it is as popular as ever. It is also excellent for anyone who is on a light diet.

1 lb. filleted smoked fish cooked in seasoned milk
1 tablespoon chopped parsley
1 oz. melted butter or margarine
2 eggs
2½ oz. fresh breadcrumbs
seasoning

Flake the cooked fish, and mix with the parsley, egg yolks and seasonings. Make up the liquid to just over ¼ pint with a little more milk if necessary. Pour it over 2 oz. of the breadcrumbs and soak for a few minutes. Stir the fish mixture together with the melted butter. Fold in stiffly whisked egg whites and transfer to greased soufflé dish. Sprinkle with the extra ½ oz. of breadcrumbs, cover with greased paper and bake for 45 minutes in a moderate oven—350°F (Gas 4).

Tweed Kettle

Potted Hough

Gaelic Steak

Cod with Cheese and Tomato

3 or 4 cod steaks cut about 1 inch thick
1–2 oz. grated cheddar cheese
salt and pepper
1 oz. margarine
1 tablespoon tomato purée

Place the cod steaks on individual squares of well-oiled aluminium foil and season with salt and pepper. Meanwhile, cream the margarine and the tomato purée together and spread generously over each cod steak. Sprinkle the grated cheese on top as thickly as possible. Wrap the cod steak up into a foil parcel. Place in a casserole and bake for about 25–30 minutes, in a fairly hot oven 375°F (Gas 5). When cooked, open the foil with care and serve the fish on a hot plate.

Cod baked with Oatmeal Balls

1 lb. cod
1 dessertspoon butter
1 breakfast cup milk
1 teacup water

Skin the fish, put it into a deep pie dish and sprinkle with a little flour. Add a little water to the milk and pour round. Put butter in little bits on the top. Bake in a hot oven basting well.

Oatmeal Balls

1 teacup oatmeal
$\frac{3}{4}$ teacup shredded suet
chopped parsley
small piece of onion
pepper and salt

Mix in a bowl oatmeal, suet, parsley, onion, pepper and salt. With a little water form into balls. Drop balls round the fish and bake for $\frac{1}{2}$ hour. The balls should be half covered with the liquid.

Cod Roe with Bacon and Tomato

Cod roe is generally fried and very good it is too. Occasionally I like to try it this way.

$\frac{1}{2}$ lb. bacon rashers to each 1 lb. of roe
2–3 tomatoes

Slice the cod roe and season with salt and pepper. Arrange in a shallow fireproof dish. Cut the bacon rashers in two and flatten with a palette knife. Spread with a little mustard and roll up tightly. Place a bacon roll on each slice of cod's roe. If any are left over, arrange them round the side of the dish with the sliced tomatoes. Bake in a moderate oven, 350°F (Gas 4), for 30 minutes.

Hairy Tatties

My mother was brought up on the farm of Waterton in Aberdeenshire and I used to spend summer holidays there with my Aunt Peggy and Uncle Jim. This was in the 1930's before fridges or deep freezes were heard of and the household depended on the fishman from Buckie or Whitehills for its weekly supply of fish. If the fishman failed to turn up my Aunt resorted to the horrid piece of dry salt cod fish which was suspended from a hook on the kitchen ceiling, and produced a dish called hairy tatties which I simply loathed, but forced down in dumb silence as there was no alternative fare; anyway, everyone was far too busy with the day-to-day running of the farm to pay much attention to any protest on my part. All the same I made a mental note to think about returning home where hairy tatties were unknown. Nevertheless, for the sake of hairy tattie addicts here is the recipe.

1 lb. salt cod fish
1 lb. cooked mashed potatoes
½ teaspoon made-up mustard
1 tablespoon finely chopped parsley
creamy milk and butter
fresh ground black pepper

Cut the fish in ½ inch slices across the grain. Soak overnight in enough tepid water to cover. Drain. Simmer in fresh boiling water for ten minutes then drain and flake, removing skin and bones. Meanwhile, drain and mash well the hot boiled potatoes. Add the flaked fish and season well with black pepper, mustard and salt if needed. Add the chopped parsley, moisten with some creamy milk and a knob of butter. Put in a dish, smooth with a knife, dot with butter and brown in the oven. Serve on a heated platter accompanied by an egg sauce. Eat with buttered oatcakes with a glass of milk to drink.

Mackerel Parcels

4 mackerel
salt
newspaper

Wash the fish and using a pair of scissors slit them down the fronts and remove the guts. Wash out the insides well. Rub salt all over the outside of each fish, wrap them in newspaper and run each parcel quickly under the cold tap. Put the fish into a moderate oven, 375°F (Gas 5), and bake for 40–45 minutes depending on their size. Not only does this method avoid any fishy smell in the kitchen but when the paper is peeled off it takes the skin as well.

Meat

As a schoolgirl I lived in the small market town of Huntly in West Aberdeenshire. My father was a farmer and apart from the townspeople most folks we knew farmed in some way or another. A busy and prosperous mart which served the farmers of this famous beef-rearing community was held every Wednesday. Then the farmers and their wives came to town to attend the mart and do the shopping. As a result we were great meat eaters and were extremely well informed about the various cuts of meat. At the butcher's shop (no pre-packed supermarket meat then!) we always asked for the meat we wanted by name. For instance, for a stew we bought shoulder steak and we always bought best quality steak mince, shin with a marrow bone for making soup, brisket or silverside for pot roasting and rib roast with a piece of the undercut for Sunday lunch. Best quality topside and ox-kidney for steak and kidney pie and of course we bought a gigot of lamb and double loin chops with the fat trimmed off. Pork was never popular in our family; in fact we rarely bought it.

Aberdeen Sausage

This is a great standby in summer. It is simple to make and has a good flavour. It is also cheap compared to other cold meat such as gammon or roast beef.

1 lb. stewing steak
½ lb. fat bacon
1 onion, peeled and sliced
4 oz. rolled oats
2 teaspoons Worcester sauce
1 level tablespoon horseradish sauce
1 beaten egg
2 tablespoons stock
black pepper
salt, if required

a little stock
browned breadcrumbs
a 1 lb. round coffee tin

Mince the steak, bacon and onion. Mix in the rolled oats, Worcester sauce, horseradish sauce, beaten egg and stock. Season the mixture with freshly ground black pepper and salt if required. Grease the inside of the tin carefully, then push the meat mixture into it, using a potato masher to avoid leaving gaps. Cover the top loosely with kitchen foil. Put tin into a roasting tin and pour boiling water round it. Bake the sausage in a moderate oven, 350°F (Gas 4), for 2 hours. When it is cooked remove the foil and pour in enough hot stock to come up to the top of the tin. Cover the sausage again with foil and put a weight on top to keep it firm. Leave it overnight.

Next day, run a knife round the inside of the tin and turn out the sausage. Scatter the browned breadcrumbs on a piece of kitchen paper, put the sausage on them and coat well. This is very good served with potato salad and baby beets.

Aberdeen

Haggis

A great deal of mystery surrounds the haggis. People either like it, dislike it or are afraid to eat it because they have been told so many weird stories about it by their Scottish 'friends'. Personally I had never eaten haggis until one day in Aberdeen I was visiting my former landlady, Mrs. Chapman, who lived in Westburn Road. She was a kind, charming woman who looked after me like a mother and I always felt part of her own family. This particular day I was visiting at lunchtime and was invited to 'draw up a chair' to the table. To my utter consternation haggis was the 'plat du jour'. I approached it rather cautiously and to my intense relief I discovered it was excellent, and I have been a great haggis-lover ever since.

I later discovered that haggis has to be properly prepared with good, fresh ingredients, otherwise it can be stodgy and fatty and sometimes quite tasteless!

To make a Haggis

To make a haggis you need the stomach bag of a sheep. Wash it well in cold water. Turn it outside in, scald and scrape it with a knife, then soak it in cold, salt water overnight. Wash the pluck (heart, liver and lights) and put into a pan of boiling water, letting the windpipe hang over the side, and add a teaspoon of salt. Allow it to boil for about 2 hours and then remove it from the pan and cut away the windpipe and any superfluous gristle.

Take a quarter of the liver and mince it along with the heart and lights. To these add about $\frac{1}{2}$ lb. chopped suet and two parboiled onions, also chopped. Toast two teacups pinhead oatmeal in the oven until golden and nutty and add to the rest of the mixture. Season well with salt and pepper (haggis is highly seasoned and some cooks add a pinch of powdered mace or cloves, although I don't care for this), then moisten with about 1 pint of the pluck or onion boilings. Drain and dry the bag and fill it three-parts full with the mixture. Room must be allowed for the oatmeal to swell, otherwise the bag will burst.

Sew the bag up with a trussing needle and coarse thread or very fine string. Prick the bag here and there with a needle and plunge the haggis into a pan with enough boiling water to cover. Place an old plate under the haggis, put on the lid and allow to boil slowly for 2 to 3 hours according to size, keeping the haggis constantly covered with water.

When cooked, remove from the pan and place on a hot plate. Remove the threads and slit open the bag. Serve steaming hot, accompanied by hot mashed potatoes and hot mashed swedes (chappit tatties and bashed neeps).

Haggis will keep for some time after it has been cooked. It can be reheated when required by putting in a saucepan of boiling water and allowing it to boil for at least an hour.

Bowl Haggis

1 sheep's pluck (liver, heart and lights)
½ lb. suet
2 large onions
1 large cup toasted pinhead oatmeal
salt and pepper

Cover the pluck with water and boil, adding water if necessary, until tender. Allow to cool in the liquid. Remove the liver, heart and lights, and mince coarsely. Chop the two onions finely. Add the cup of toasted oatmeal and moisten with the liquid in which the pluck was boiled. Put in a bowl and press down lightly. Cover with greaseproof paper and foil and steam for 4 hours.

Any Day Scotch Haggis

This recipe is very good if you prefer to miss out all the tedious preparation of 'real haggis' and it is surprising how like the real thing it is. I make it quite often as I like its texture, which is light, and the flavour is very savoury. It is also most economical and the quantities below will feed five people. Serve with the traditional accompaniments of mashed potatoes and swedes.

½ lb. ox liver
4 oz. shredded suet
4 oz. pinhead oatmeal
1 onion (5 oz.)
freshly ground black pepper
salt

Place liver in a small saucepan with the onion and add one teacup water. Boil for 15 minutes. Meanwhile, toast the oatmeal for a few minutes in the oven till light brown. Mince the liver and onion and make the liquid up to a cup with water. Mix all together with seasoning and liquid. I use about ¾ level dessertspoon of salt and a generous sprinkling of black pepper. Turn into a greased bowl, cover and steam for 2 hours.

Forfar Bridies

These are great specialities in Angus and are the Scottish equivalent of Cornish pasties.

1 lb. topside or shoulder steak
3 oz. shredded suet
2 tablespoons minced onion
salt and pepper
1 lb. rough puff or flaky pastry

Beat the meat well with a rolling pin and cut into thin strips about 1 inch long. If a cheaper cut of meat is used, mince it. Roll the pastry out about ¼-inch thick and cut it into three equal-sized rounds or ovals. Mix the meat with the suet and the onion and season with salt and pepper. Cover half of each oval with one-third of the meat. Brush the edges with water, fold over, and crimp with finger and thumb, cut a small hole on the top of each to allow the steam to escape. Bake in a hot oven, 450°F (Gas 8), for about 15 minutes, then lower the heat to 350°F (Gas 4) and bake until steak is tender, about one hour. Serve hot or cold.

Potted Hough

This is another Scottish traditional recipe. It must be eaten cold with salad or boiled potatoes.

2½–3 lb. hough
1 nap bone
salt and freshly ground black pepper
pinch dried herbs—if desired
cold water to cover

Rinse the hough and the nap bone. Place in a saucepan, and cover with cold water. Add a teaspoon of salt. Bring slowly to the boil. Simmer very gently for 5–6 hours, then remove all the bones. Strain the meat and place on a board. Mince finely. Return to stock. Add salt and freshly ground black pepper to taste, and the herbs. Bring quickly to the boil. Boil for about 8 minutes. Remove pan from stove. Leave until nearly cold, then stir and set in wet basins or moulds.

Mince Collops

Haggis is regarded as being the national dish of Scotland, but I think if the Scots were asked to name their favourite dish it would be mince by a long way. Most people have mince at least once a week. It is used as a savoury dish and I find that a generous assortment of finely diced fresh onions, carrots and swedes added to the minced beef greatly improves the flavour. Mince is always served up with mashed potatoes and swedes or cabbage, and of course it is often accompanied by mealy puddings, sometimes placed on the top of the mince in the pan to heat through.

1 lb. best quality minced steak
2–3 carrots, diced
½–¾ pint hot water
1 large onion, chopped
about 1–2 oz. beef dripping
serve with sippets of toast

Heat the dripping in a heavy-bottomed stew pan over a strong heat. When it is melted and really hot put in the mince and allow to seal and brown nicely, about 5–10 minutes, then add the onion and carrot, and season. Reduce the heat to low and add enough water to cover the mince. Allow to simmer slowly for about 1–1½ hours until the mince is cooked and most of the liquid evaporated. Stir from time to time. Serve with mashed potatoes and mashed swedes seasoned with plenty of salt and pepper and beaten up with a good lump of butter or a little thin cream.

I never add flour or oatmeal to thicken, as is traditionally done, as I think this spoils the flavour of the meat.

Gaelic Steaks

2 tablespoons oil
2 oz. butter
1 onion, peeled and finely chopped (optional)
4 fillet steaks
1 clove garlic (optional)
salt and black pepper
2–4 tablespoons whisky
2 tablespoons chopped parsley

Heat oil and butter in a frying pan. Add onion and fry gently till soft and just beginning to brown. Rub steaks with cut surface of garlic and season well. Fry steaks for 2–5 minutes each side depending whether rare or well done is preferred. Pour on whisky (flame if desired) and add parsley and salt and pepper to taste. Turn steaks over once and spoon juices over for about ½ minute. Serve immediately with fresh French beans or salad and sauté potatoes.

Small Mutton Pies

Mutton pies seem to have lost their popularity. In the 1920's and 1930's they were in every baker's shop but now I rarely see them. The steak mince pie has completely taken over.

1 lb. lean mutton or lamb (leg or shoulder)
3 onions
¼ level teaspoon pepper
2 tablespoons chopped parsley
1 level teaspoon salt
flour to thicken (2 level tablespoons per ½ pint of stock)
¾ lb. shortcrust pastry

Cut or mince the meat into small pieces. Peel and chop the onions. Make the pastry while the meat cooks. Put meat, onion and seasoning in a pan with water barely to cover, and simmer slowly until the meat is tender. Blend the flour with a little cold water and use to thicken the liquid. Add the chopped parsley and cool. Roll the pastry and cut into rounds to line small bun tins and an equal number of rounds for the tops. Put a little of the mixture in each pastry case, cut a hole in the top pieces, put them on and seal the edges. Brush with egg or milk and bake until brown. Serve hot or cold.

Scalloped Scotch Beef

$\frac{1}{2}$ lb. onions, sliced
1 lb. minced beef
4 oz. mushrooms, sliced
1 level tablespoon cornflour
1 level teaspoon salt
$\frac{1}{8}$ level teaspoon pepper
2 tablespoons water
little gravy browning
1$\frac{1}{2}$ lb. peeled potatoes
$\frac{3}{4}$ pint water
$\frac{1}{2}$ oz. lard or dripping

Put onions in a 3-pint ovenproof casserole with the minced beef, then the mushrooms, on top. Blend the cornflour and seasoning with 2 tablespoons of water, add gravy browning and stir into meat. Pour over $\frac{3}{4}$ pint water, slice the potatoes and arrange over the top. Dot with fat. Cover and bake 350°F (Gas 4) for about two hours. Remove the lid 20 to 25 minutes before serving, to brown potatoes.

Grannie Downie's Mince Pudding

This was a favourite recipe of my grandmother, who lived in Strathdon. The family lived off the farm, with its plentiful fresh vegetables, chickens, milk and oatmeal. Indeed, the visit to the butcher was something of an occasion as they had ample supplies of game from the moors, and fresh fish from the River Don.

$\frac{1}{2}$ lb. raw minced beef
1 teacup self-raising flour
1 teacup fresh breadcrumbs
1 medium sized potato, grated
1 medium sized carrot, grated
salt and pepper

1 level teaspoon powdered herbs
water, if required

Mix all the ingredients together, adding water only if necessary to make a soft paste. Turn the mixture into four or five greased moulds or cups, tie a round of greased paper over the top and steam until firm—45 minutes to 1 hour. Turn out and serve with gravy and a green vegetable.

Scotch Eggs

Scotch eggs are popular everywhere, not only in Scotland. They are delicious with salads and are very much enjoyed as a lunchtime snack with a glass of beer or lager.

5 eggs
1 lb. pork sausage meat
½ teaspoon salt
2 oz. brown breadcrumbs
fat or oil for deep frying
large pinch pepper

Boil four of the eggs for 12 minutes until hard. Remove the shells and cool in cold water. Mix together flour, salt and pepper and sprinkle on to a board. Divide sausage meat into four on floured board and flatten into round cakes large enough to cover eggs. Dip eggs into flour and wrap sausage cakes around each egg to completely encase them. Flatten the end so that they will stand upright. Lightly whisk the remaining egg. Put crumbs on to foil. Brush the eggs with whisked egg, then toss in the crumbs, pressing crumbs well in. Heat the fat until hot. Carefully lower the Scotch eggs into the fat. Cook for about 5 minutes. Remove and drain well on kitchen paper. Serve hot or cold. Serves four.

Market Day Casserole

The busiest housewife will find the following recipe most useful as it will look after itself, and the longer the cooking the more savoury the dish will be.

1½–2 lb. potatoes
1 small apple
2 pig's kidneys
3 medium sized onions
6 pork chops
seasoning
pinch of crushed, dried sage

Peel and slice the potatoes and place in layers in a strong, fireproof dish with the chops, sliced kidneys, sliced apple, seasoning and sage, finishing with a layer of potatoes. Pour over one teacup of water, cover with a tightly fitting lid and cook slowly for 3 hours.

Game

Scotland is a wonderful natural larder of game. The red deer from the hilltops provides fine venison, the hare and the pheasant, the partridge and the grouse—what infinite variety! And yet so little is known about the art of cooking game. I have always lived in the country and someone has always been handy with a gun to provide something for the pot, but to city dwellers the succulent roast venison, hare pâté, or pheasant casserole are something of a mystery. In this chapter I have given a few quite simple recipes which are easy to follow.

Grouse Pudding

This is an excellent method of using an old bird.

1 grouse
½ lb. stewing steak
1 oz. flour
¼ pint stock
1 hard-boiled egg, sliced
salt and pepper
12 oz. suet crust pastry
chopped onion
¼ teaspoon dried mixed herbs

Cut the flesh from the bird and the steak into small pieces. Dip them in the seasoned flour. Make a suet pastry and line a greased basin with ⅔ of it. Put in the meat, sliced eggs, onion, mixed herbs and the stock. Cover with the remainder of the pastry. Make a hole in the lid, cover with greased paper and steam at least 3 hours.

Roast Grouse

Only young, well hung grouse are suitable for roasting, and properly cooked and served they make a true gourmet meal. Wipe the grouse inside and out with a

Grouse shooting

damp cloth but do not wash them. Put an ounce or two
of butter, into which you have worked a little lemon
juice, salt and pepper, into each grouse. Wrap them in
fat bacon and roast at 425°F (Gas 7) for about 25–30
minutes according to the size of the birds, basting
occasionally. Grouse should not be overcooked, and
must be removed from the oven in the nick of time.
Meanwhile, simmer the livers in water for about 10
minutes and pound them in a bowl with a little butter,
salt and cayenne and spread this on pieces of bread
which have been toasted on one side only.

Place the roast grouse on the bread croutes and serve
with fried crumbs and potato crisps. Garnish with
watercress and hand round cranberry sauce and bread
sauce.

Burns Supper showing Haggis, Bashed Neeps & Chappit Tatties

To Serve with Game Birds

Buttered Crumbs are made by heating ½ oz. butter or 1 tablespoon of the fat in which the game birds were roasted, in a frying pan, then adding one teacup of fresh white breadcrumbs. Stir and fry slowly till light brown. Season with salt and pepper to taste.

Gravy Pour off the fat from the roasting tin and add a little boiling water to the gravy. Add a good pinch of salt with a teaspoon of grated orange or lemon rind added to sharpen the flavour, and return the tin to the oven to reduce a little.

Grouse, partridge and pheasant can all be roasted providing they are young birds. Older birds make excellent casseroles.

Gamekeepers' Stew

brace of grouse (old)
4 oz. dripping
2 or 3 tomatoes
1 onion
a few peppercorns
2 rashers streaky bacon
4 oz. mushrooms
salt and pepper
4 cloves

Cut the prepared birds in half and fry all over in a heavy frying pan with sufficient dripping to brown them lightly. Then transfer to a heated casserole and add the tomatoes, cut in half, and the onions, quartered, and stuck with cloves. Put in all the other ingredients and add just enough water to cover. Put on the lid and cook in a moderate oven, 350°F (Gas 4), for 2 hours until tender. When nearly ready add a little thickening and browning to the liquid in the dish.

Roast Grouse

Pheasant Normande

My husband and I were once invited to give a Baxter lunch for the food and beverage managers of the Hilton Hotels in Europe at the Paris Hilton. The menu was:

Wild Duck Consommé
Pheasant Normande
Purée of Celery and Cranberry Stuffed Apples
Tipsy Laird

This is the recipe we used for pheasant Normande.

1 pheasant
1 lb. cooking apples
4–5 tablespoons single cream
2 oz. melted butter
2 oz. sliced mushrooms
salt and pepper

Prepare the bird and melt the butter in a strong pan. Brown the pheasant evenly all over. Peel, core and slice the apples. Layer half the apples in a $2\frac{1}{2}$ pint casserole. Pour a little butter over the apples and put in the pheasant. Surround with the rest of the apples and the mushrooms, seasoning each layer. Pour over the rest of the butter and cream. Cover tightly and cook in the oven at 350°F (Gas 4) for about 1 hour. Serves four.

Roast Wild Duck

To remove the fishy taste of wild duck, cover a deep roasting tin to a depth of $\frac{1}{2}$ inch with boiling water. Add 1 tablespoon salt. Put in the bird and bake it for 10 minutes, basting frequently with the salt water. Drain. Sprinkle lightly with flour, baste well with hot butter and roast in a moderate oven, 350°F (Gas 4), for 20–30 minutes, basting frequently. The birds should always be served rather underdone. Serve with a port wine sauce and orange salad.

Port wine sauce

1 tablespoon red currant jelly
$\frac{1}{8}$ pint port wine
$\frac{1}{4}$ pint good game or mutton stock

Heat all the ingredients together until the jelly is melted.

Hunters Casserole

$1\frac{1}{2}$–2 lb. rabbit joints
6 rashers streaky bacon
3 onions
1 pint stock
1 coarsely grated carrot
$\frac{1}{2}$ teaspoon mixed herbs
salt and pepper

Trim the rabbit joints. Peel and slice the onions. Fill casserole with layers of rabbit, bacon, onions, sprinkling mixed herbs and seasoning between each layer. Pour stock over. Cover and cook in a moderately slow oven, 335°F (Gas 3), for $1\frac{1}{2}$ hours. Stir in carrot and return to oven for further 30 minutes.

Venison Casserole

Venison is an acquired taste, particularly for city dwellers, where it is difficult to obtain in the shops. I think if you are given a piece by some of your country friends the best way to cook it is in a casserole. Red deer tends to be tougher and needs longer cooking. Roe deer is more tender.

2 lb. roe venison haunch
2 oz. dripping
2 onions
3 carrots
2 oz. bacon

1 oz. flour
1 gill red wine
1 gill beef stock
salt and pepper
bouquet garni
pinch garlic powder
spray of rosemary
pinch of allspice
two tablespoons red currant jelly

Brown meat in the dripping in a heavy frying pan. Put it aside. Fry onions, carrots and bacon with a pinch of sugar to brown them. Remove the vegetables. Add the flour to the pan to thicken, then stir in the stock and the wine. Put the venison in the casserole with the vegetables and seasonings and pour the liquid over it. Cook in a moderate oven for $2\frac{1}{2}$ hours. Add two tablespoons red currant jelly about 10 minutes before serving and mix it well into the liquid.

Venison Roast in Foil

joint of venison
dripping
flour

Venison is a very dry meat and has to be marinated for at least 24 hours before cooking. I think the marinade procedure tends to put people off cooking venison, but it is very simple.

Marinade

You require a thinly sliced carrot and onion, a bay leaf, a crushed clove of garlic, parsley stalks, crushed peppercorns and salt, $\frac{1}{2}$ cup of oil, $\frac{3}{4}$ pint of red wine. Mix together in a deep casserole. Place the venison in the marinade and soak, turning from time to time.

Remove from the marinade and dry with a towel, then rub the meat all over with the dripping, giving a good coating, and wrap in greaseproof paper. Then wrap in foil like a parcel. Roast in a moderate oven, 350°F (Gas 4), for 20 minutes to the pound. Half an hour before serving, remove the coverings and dredge with flour, increase the heat of the oven and baste well. Serve with gravy and cranberry sauce.

Venison Mince Collops

These recipes for venison mince collops and venison paste were sent to me by a friend who lived on an estate on the West Coast of Scotland for many years.

1 lb. venison mince
1 onion, chopped and sautéed till transparent
4 oz. fresh white breadcrumbs
salt and pepper
1 egg

Mix all well together and form into balls. Roll in seasoned flour and brown well in some dripping. Add stock and seasoning and simmer for about an hour. Thicken gravy if liked.

Venison Paste

1 lb. venison cut in pieces (odd trimmings will do)
¼ pint stock
1 clove
pinch thyme
mace
salt and pepper

Put all the ingredients into a casserole and cover. Bake in a moderate oven for 2½ hours at least, till very tender. Put into liquidiser, moisten with 1 oz. melted butter and some red wine, and mix to a good consistency. If a finer mixture is required, pound paste in a bowl and sieve. Marvellous as a filling for sandwiches or on hot buttered toast.

Game Pâté

Pâté is such a popular dish at the moment I feel I must give the recipe for this game pâté. It is an excellent pâté and freezes well.

6–8 oz. boned hare or pigeon plus liver
8 oz. belly pork
2 rashers back bacon
3 oz. hard pork fat
2 oz. rump steak
1 egg, beaten
½ slice of bread, crumbled
3 oz. chopped onion
2 oz. butter
parsley and thyme, finely chopped, or a good pinch of mixed dried herbs
large clove garlic
1 liqueur glass cognac or wine

Dice the hard pork fat and half the game. Finely mince the rest of the game, liver, pork belly, bacon and steak. Simmer the onion and crushed garlic in the butter for 10 minutes without browning them, and add, along with the breadcrumbs, herbs, beaten egg and alcohol, to the pâté (don't stint the herbs), season with salt and pepper. Mix everything well with your hands.

Pack into a buttered 1 pint terrine or 2 small ones. Cover with a double layer of kitchen foil, stand in a pan of hot water and bake for 1–1½ hours, 310°F (Gas 2). Leave to cool without disturbing the lid. Keep for two days for the flavour to develop.

Hare Pâté

This pâté makes a good start for a dinner party and serves eight.

1 hare
1 teaspoon mixed fresh herbs
$\frac{1}{4}$ lb. pork liver
1 clove garlic
3–4 thin rashers fat bacon
$\frac{1}{4}$ pint red wine
$\frac{1}{2}$ lb. belly pork
salt and freshly ground black pepper
2 tablespoons brandy
about $\frac{1}{2}$ pint strained jellied stock (made from hare bones or aspic jelly)

Wipe the hare with a clean damp cloth, then cut away the meat with a sharp knife. Place the best pieces of meat in a dish, pour over the red wine and herbs and leave to marinate for a few hours. Mince the remaining hare, belly of pork and liver. Mix in salt and pepper, crushed garlic and brandy. Moisten with red wine and herbs drained from the hare pieces. Rub a $1\frac{1}{2}$ pint size terrine with fat and line the base with the fat bacon, fill with the minced mixture and prepared pieces of hare. Cover with a lid or foil and stand in a baking dish filled with water to reach halfway up the dish. Cook in a moderate oven, 350°F (Gas 4), for $2\frac{1}{4}$–$2\frac{1}{2}$ hours till cooked through. Drain off liquid and top up the dish with the strained jellied stock or aspic. Allow to set and turn out.

Traditional

At dinner time the farming folk throughout the North East would say—'Well, I'll awa hame tae ma tatties.'

In Scotland potatoes are a basic vegetable used many ways—the following three recipes show regional differences in the use of potato.

Clapshot (Orkney)

1 lb. potatoes
1 lb. turnips
1 dessertspoon finely chopped chives
lump of butter or dripping
salt and black pepper

Boil the potatoes and turnips and mash them together. Add the chives, butter or dripping and salt and fresh ground black pepper to taste. Mix thoroughly and serve very hot. A marvellous accompaniment to haggis.

The Orkneys

Colcannon (North East & Aberdeenshire) or Kailkenny (Highland)

> 1 lb. cold boiled potatoes
> 1 lb. cold boiled cabbage
> 2 oz. butter
> ½ teaspoon salt
> ½ teaspoon pepper

Mash the potatoes, chop the cold cabbage and mix with the potatoes. Turn into a saucepan. Beat in the butter, salt and pepper. Stir over a low heat until the fat is melted and blended with the vegetables. Serve with cold lamb or mutton.

In some parts of Scotland, the colcannon is put into a greased pie dish and baked in a hot oven for about 25 minutes.

Rumbledethumps (Borders)

This is the name people in the Borders give to a dish very similar to colcannon. Chopped chives or cooked onions are sometimes added. The mixture may be put in a greased pie dish, covered with grated cheese and baked in a hot oven till brown on top.

Stovies

To use the last of roast meat.

> 2 lb. potatoes and 1 onion
> ½ pint hot water or stock made from drippings in roasting tin
> scraps of roast beef or lamb
> 2 oz. butter and dripping mixed
> salt and pepper

Melt the fat in a stewpan. Peel and thickly slice the potatoes and onion into the pan. Toss in the fat for a few minutes. Add the stock or water, salt and pepper. Cover and bring slowly to the boil. Simmer gently, stirring occasionally to prevent sticking, for an hour. Add the scraps of roast meat and cook a little longer until the potatoes are slightly brown and the meat is hot. Serve with a generous handful of freshly chopped parsley. Oatcakes and a glass of milk are the traditional accompaniments to this good old Scots' rib-sticking dish.

Bashed Neeps

1 large swede cut after frost
1 oz. butter
salt and freshly ground black pepper
pinch of grated nutmeg

Cut the swede into large dice. Put into a saucepan and cover with cold water. Add a level teaspoon salt. Cover and simmer until the swedes are tender. (Keep a careful eye on them as they tend to boil in easily, and I have pan to prove it.) Mash till smooth, then put in a blender and add the butter, nutmeg, salt and pepper. Sometimes I add a tablespoon of cream which transforms this vegetable into a dish fit for a queen. Serve very hot. This is the way to cook traditional bashed neeps to serve with haggis.

Kail (rich in iron and vitamins)

A new doctor announced he was leaving a Highland village, and when asked why, he explained it was because there were too many kail yards and consequently too few patients. It is a favourite vegetable of the country people and withstands the most severe winter. Kail, always referred to as 'them', is really most delicious cooked in the way I describe. It is similar to creamed spinach and accompanies any hot meat dish, even hamburgers.

large bunch of green kail
1 tablespoon cream
oatmeal
pepper and salt
water

Kail 'boils away' very quickly, so enough to fill a medium sized saucepan is needed. Wash the kail and remove the hard ribbing. Place in a pan and cover with boiling water. Boil till tender, leaving pan uncovered.

Strain kail and place in a blender with some of the strained liquid. Purée. Return kail to pan and sprinkle with a little oatmeal. Add the cream, salt and pepper to taste. Stir, boil up for a few minutes, and serve.

The oatmeal may be omitted if desired.

Kail Brose

When I was a schoolgirl during the Second World War, food was severely rationed and even the farming communities had a difficult time. Meat was in short supply and we were glad of a tin of Spam or corned beef—in fact such things were considered something of a luxury and available only when there were enough points coupons to exchange for them. My mother fell back on old-fashioned recipes used by my grandmother, such as kail and kail brose, stovies, chappit tatties and skirlie. So we managed on a rather dull and monotonous diet, but nevertheless very nutritious fare.

In Aberdeenshire our mid-week lunch was kail brose in winter time. I must admit it wasn't my favourite meal but I was hungry and in a hurry to get back to school. It consisted of a bowl of oatmeal brose made as follows:

1 lb. hough or a nap bone
oatmeal
salt
water

Put the meat and the bone into a pan and cover with cold water and a good pinch of salt. Boil for at least an hour but longer if possible. Lightly toast a handful of oatmeal by spreading it on a baking tray and leaving it in a hot oven for a few minutes until it is nutty and dry. Put the oatmeal into a bowl with a good pinch of salt, dash in a ladleful of the boiling hot broth and stir vigorously to a smooth consistency.

This was accompanied by the puréed kail which was served in a small porridge plate. A spoonful of kail was dipped into the brose and the two eaten together and swilled down with a glass of fresh milk.

Skirlie and Chappit Tatties

Saturday was skirlie day. As everyone was busy with their own activities on Saturday, my mother gave up in despair of trying to get us all together for lunch, so a huge pan of skirlie sat on the top of the stove and it was self-service from then on.

oatmeal
roast fat
1 or 2 onions
salt and pepper

Have a thick-bottomed stewpan very hot and put in the fat to melt. Add the finely chopped onions and brown them well—this adds to the flavour of the skirlie. Now sprinkle in the oatmeal stirring all the time, until the fat is absorbed; a fairly stiff mixture. Season well with salt and pepper and stir until the skirlie is thoroughly cooked—about 5–10 minutes. Serve with chappit (mashed) potatoes.

Porridge

One of Dr. Johnson's famous quotations tells us: 'Oats. A grain, which in England is generally given to horses, but in Scotland supports the people.' Poor fellow, he was sorely prejudiced. Nourishing, rich in vitamins, accompanied by a bowl of creamy milk, it has indeed sustained generations of hardy Scots.

My brother, Tom, and I always had porridge before going to school and it was a proper bother to make. It was of course made from oatmeal and took about half an hour to cook. Sometimes it boiled over or sometimes it had 'knots', as we called lumps of meal, in it, or it was too hot. However, it was usually poured into plates (we each had our own jealously guarded plate) and was nicely cool and set ready for us to eat when we came downstairs. The night before, the milk was set out into individual bowls and by morning had a lovely head of cream on it. We took a spoonful of porridge and dipped it into the bowl of milk and ate it in this time-honoured fashion. We also had a spoonful of golden syrup plunged into the middle of the porridge. This gave it a lovely sweetness which we adored. Occasionally we used to have great fun 'writing' our names from a spoonful of syrup held aloft. Of course we both had short names, Tom and Ena, so it was easy.

1 pint cold water
2 oz. medium oatmeal
salt

Bring the water to a rolling boil and add a level teaspoon of salt. Take the oatmeal and sprinkle slowly into the water, keeping it on the boil and stirring constantly. Half cover the pan with the lid and turn down the heat to low. Stir frequently and simmer gently until the meal swells and the porridge is thick and creamy—about 30 minutes. Taste and add more salt if required. If the porridge is too thick, add extra boiling water.

Mealy

> *2 teacups pinhead oatmeal*
> *1 small onion or shallot, finely chopped*
> *1 oz. butter, 1 oz. lard, mixed*
> *salt and pepper*

Mix all ingredients together and put in a bowl. Cover and steam 1–1½ hours. Leave enough room at the top of the bowl to allow the oatmeal to swell. Use as a stuffing for chicken or turkey or serve with mince and tatties.

Mealy Puddings

These keep well, especially if stored in oatmeal.

> *2 lb. oatmeal*
> *1 lb. shredded suet*
> *2 onions*
> *salt and pepper*
> *pudding skins*

Soak skins in salted water, then rinse well in cold water. Toast the oatmeal lightly in the oven. Mince the onions. Add onions and suet to the meal, with salt and pepper to taste. Mix well. Fill the mixture into skins (not too full to allow oatmeal to swell). Tie ends and drop into boiling water. Prick occasionally with fork to prevent bursting. Cook steadily. When required, boil again until heated through.

Crowdie Salad

My father was a dairy farmer and consequently there was always plenty of milk in our household. In summer my mother used to make crowdie and serve it with salad. Sometimes we spread great heaps of it on oatcakes and ate it for tea.

To make crowdie cheese, turn a pint of sour milk into a pan, add a squeeze of lemon juice and beat until a curd is formed. Drain in buttermuslin and hang up to drip for several hours. When thoroughly drained, chop the curd roughly, adding salt to taste, and pack into a bowl. To make the salad, put the crowdie into the centre of a round platter and surround with shredded lettuce, cucumber and cress. Dust the top of the crowdie with paprika pepper or sprinkle with some chopped chives or parsley.

Haggis Balls

These savoury little haggis balls are made to my own recipe concocted on the spur of the moment. Our family firm, 'Baxters of Speyside', was invited to take part in a British Trade Fortnight promotion in the famous Macy's department store in New York. Prior to this the publicity manager from Macys (a lady) arrived, one snowy January weekend, to absorb the atmosphere of Speyside. My husband, Gordon, put on a good show and took her on a tour of the snow-covered countryside, including a pheasant shoot, where she was a guest at the shooters' lunch which took place amongst bales of straw in a Banffshire farm tractor-shed. Dressed up in her mink coat and my fur-lined boots she had a hilarious time and thought Scotland was just the greatest 'little ole country'. As she was seeing it through a haze of malt whisky and hot pies, I am not altogether surprised. In the evening we gave a small party for her and I decided to serve haggis in some form or other, so I made these haggis balls which we ate as a hot *hors d'oeuvres* with drams of whisky and they were an instant success.

Now, when my husband and I are promoting our

products the world over, we serve haggis balls. They are always popular and people seem to be so excited to have tasted and eaten the notorious beast at last. To make them you will need:

1 tin of Baxters Scotch haggis
1 egg
roast fat for deep frying
breadcrumbs

Empty haggis into a mixing bowl, add the yolk of egg and mix well together. Take teaspoonfuls of the mixture and roll into balls about the size of marbles. Don't make them too big as they are eaten in one bite. Dip into the lightly beaten egg white, roll in breadcrumbs and deep fry until crisp and brown. Drain well, insert cocktail sticks and serve hot.

Stoorum

oatmeal
water
salt
milk

Put a heaped tablespoon of oatmeal into a tumbler, pour a little cold water over it and stir well. Fill up half-way with boiling water, then to the top with boiling milk. Season with salt and serve.

Atholl Brose

oatmeal
heather honey, drained
cream
water
whisky

Beat $1\frac{1}{2}$ teacups double cream to a floppy consistency.

Venison Casserole

Colcannon & Kail Brose

Stir in 1 teacup of lightly toasted oatmeal (for method for toasting oatmeal see p. 56), add half a cup of drained heather honey, and just before serving add two wine glasses of whisky. Mix thoroughly and serve in shallow glasses or small thistle-shaped glasses. I serve this as a dessert; it is really a type of Scottish syllabub.

Brochan (A bed-time drink)

Put two heaped tablespoons oatmeal into a bowl. Pour over 1 pint milk and stir well. Add ½ cupful boiling water and stir again. Leave standing for 1 hour, stirring now and again. Pour off liquid into a saucepan and bring almost to boiling point, stirring all the time. Sweeten to taste with comb honey if possible.

Auld Man's Milk

This is a kind of Scotch Advocaat.

2 standard eggs, separated
½ pint milk
2 oz. caster sugar
4 tablespoons whisky
a little grated nutmeg

Whisk egg yolks with sugar until thick and creamy. Whisk egg whites until stiff. Whisk milk and whisky into egg yolk mixture. Add nutmeg. Carefully fold in egg whites. Pour into glasses and serve at once.

Granny's Clootie Dumpling

1 lb. self-raising flour
1 lb. raisins
½ lb. suet
3 teaspoons mixed spice
½ lb. granulated sugar
1 teaspoon baking soda

$\frac{1}{2}$ teaspoon salt
3 tablespoons treacle (optional)
milk

Mix all the ingredients together and add enough milk to make a stiff dough. Dip a pudding cloth into boiling water. Sink it in a basin large enough to hold the dough. Dredge with flour and spoon in the dough mix. The bowl gives it a round shape. Draw the fullness of the cloth together evenly, then tie it tightly with string but leave enough room for the dumpling to swell. Place a plate in the bottom of a large saucepan. Lift the dumpling into the pan. Pour in enough boiling water to cover. Simmer for fully 3 hours. Turn out carefully on to a hot serving dish. Dredge with caster sugar and serve with hot custard sauce.

Scotch Black Bun

8 oz. shortcrust pastry
8 oz. flour
$\frac{1}{2}$ teaspoon baking powder
$\frac{1}{4}$ teaspoon black pepper
1 teaspoon ground ginger
1 teaspoon ground cloves
2 eggs
4 oz. soft brown sugar
1 lb. raisins
1 lb. currants
2 oz. chopped candied peel
2 oz. almonds, blanched, chopped
1 peeled, cored and grated apple

Grease an 8-inch cake tin and line with greaseproof paper. Roll out pastry thinly and line prepared tin (keep enough pastry to cover top). Sieve the flour, baking powder, pepper, ginger and cloves into a bowl. Stir in sugar, fruit, peel and grated apple. Mix in beaten eggs and bind ingredients thoroughly together. Turn into tin, and fit top. Make four holes right through to the bottom with a skewer. Bake in a moderate oven for 3 hours.

Aberdeen Buttery Rowies

1 lb. flour
1 oz. bakers yeast ($\frac{1}{2}$ tablespoon dried yeast)
1 level tablespoon salt
$\frac{1}{2}$ pint lukewarm water
6 oz. lard
6 oz. butter or margarine
1 level tablespoon caster sugar

Warm the mixing bowl and cooking utensils to be used. This is necessary when working with yeast. Sieve the flour in mixing bowl. Mix yeast, salt and sugar and add to the flour along with the lukewarm water. Mix together and set in a warm place to rise until twice its bulk, keeping it covered with a warm damp towel while it proves. Beat fats until blended, then divide fats into three equal parts. Roll out dough into a strip on a floured board. Dot the first part of the fat over it in small pats. Fold in three and roll out as for flaky pastry. Repeat twice until fat is used up. Divide into oval bun shapes. Put a little apart on a greased and floured tray and prove in a warm place for another thirty minutes, then bake in a fairly hot oven, 400°F (Gas 6), for 20–25 minutes. Reduce the heat a little as the rolls cook.

Desserts

Strathmore Strawberry Shortcake

8 oz. salted butter
4 oz. caster sugar
8 oz. plain flour
4 oz. ground almonds
a few drops almond essence
1 beaten egg white
1–2 oz. caster sugar
2 oz. flaked almonds
1 lb. strawberries
1 pint rich custard sauce

Cream the butter and 4 oz. caster sugar together, add flour gradually, together with ground almonds and almond essence. Knead the mixture until smooth and free from cracks. Roll the mixture out on a lightly floured board to form two rounds about 8 inches in diameter. Place in lightly greased 8-inch sandwich tins and smooth tops with a palette knife. Brush tops with beaten egg white and sprinkle with a little caster sugar and flaked almonds. Bake in a moderate oven (350°F, Gas 4) for 20–30 minutes. Remove from oven and cool on rack.

To assemble—arrange a layer of strawberries in base of dish. Place a round of shortcake on top. Cover with more strawberries, pour over custard, reserving two tablespoons for top. Put remaining shortcake in position, spoon custard into middle and decorate with remaining strawberries. Serves eight to ten.

Tipsy Laird

6 stale sponge cakes or swiss roll
1 jar raspberry jam
finely grated rind of a lemon
1 gill sherry
2 tablespoons brandy

½ pint double cream
caster sugar
vanilla flavouring
1 pint rich custard sauce

Split the sponge cakes and spread thickly with the jam and arrange in a glass bowl. If using swiss roll, cut into slices and arrange along the bottom and sides of a glass compote dish. Sprinkle with finely grated lemon rind. Mix the sherry and brandy together and pour over the sponge cake, allowing it to soak in throughly. Pour over the custard and allow to stand until cold and firm. Whip the cream until floppy, add caster sugar to taste, and a few drops of vanilla flavouring. Pile this over the top of the custard and decorate the top with glacé cherries and angelica or chopped nuts.

Strathbogie Mist

2 oz. caster sugar
juice of ½ a lemon
⅛ pint Crabbies ginger wine
4 pear halves (tinned)
grated rind of ½ a lemon
½ pint double cream

Mash the pears lightly with a fork and place in the base of individual glass dishes. Stir together the sugar, lemon juice, rind and Crabbies ginger wine until the sugar has dissolved. Add the cream and whip lightly. Pile on top of the pears and serve chilled. Serves three or four.

School Holiday Pudding

So called because it doesn't mind waiting and is filling enough to satisfy even the heartiest appetites.

8 oz. flour
grated rind of 1 orange

3 oz. caster sugar
pinch of salt
2 level teaspoons baking powder
4 oz. chopped figs
4 oz. chopped dates
4 oz. margarine or shredded suet
milk to mix

Sift together the flour, salt and baking powder into a mixing bowl. Add the margarine or suet, sugar, figs, dates and the orange rind, finely grated. Moisten the ingredients with milk to the consistency of a thick batter and turn into a buttered bowl. Cover the bowl closely and steam the pudding for 2½ hours.

Mrs. Fettes' Plum Pudding

This is the recipe used by my housekeeper, Mrs. Fettes. My children loved this pudding and when small often helped to prepare it by grating the carrots and squeezing the lemon. I still make it for my Christmas pudding as it is full of flavour and yet not at all heavy or difficult to digest.

4 oz. self-raising flour
pinch of salt
half a nutmeg, grated
4 oz. sugar
4 oz. shredded suet
4 oz. currants
4 oz. sultanas
2 oz. chopped peel
4 oz. grated carrot
grated rind and juice of one lemon
2 eggs beaten with a little milk

Mix all the ingredients together and stir thoroughly until the consistency of a thick batter. Steam in a well-greased pudding basin for 2–3 hours.

Butter-Scotch Pie

Strictly speaking, this is not a pie but a tart. A pie has pastry above its contents, a tart has pastry below. The favourite tart in Scotland as in England and America and probably all over the world is made with apples. There is the story of the small Glasgow boy who looked over the well-laden table of his Auntie Jessie, made a wry face and exclaimed: 'Nae Aipple Tairt! It's no' a pairty if there's nae aipple tairt.' Here is a change from Aipple Tairt:

1 teacup brown sugar
4 level tablespoons flour
1 teacup milk
4 tablespoons water
2 oz. butter
1 teaspoon vanilla essence
1 egg
6 oz. shortcrust pastry

Line a tart plate with the pastry and bake blind. Mix the sugar and flour and blend with the water. Bring the milk to boiling point and pour over. Add the butter and mix well. Stir over a low heat and add vanilla essence and egg yolk. Stir well and pour into pastry case. Make a meringue with the white of egg and $1\frac{1}{2}$ oz. caster sugar. Pile on top and brown lightly in a slow oven.

Apple and Bramble Pie (Illustrated on the cover)

1 lb. rich shortcrust pastry
$\frac{1}{2}$ lb. cooking apples
$\frac{1}{2}$ lb. brambles (wild blackberries)
3 oz. sugar
$\frac{3}{4}$ oz. cornflour

Divide the pastry into two balls, one slightly larger than the other. Roll out the smaller ball to about 8 inches in diameter and about $\frac{1}{4}$ inch thick. Put on a baking sheet and chill in the fridge. Roll out the larger ball to about 11 inches in diameter and fit into a 9-inch loose-bottomed flan ring, pressing well in. Cut off the excess pastry with a rolling pin and use to make pastry leaves for decoration.

Peel, core and slice the apples and put them in a saucepan with the brambles and the sugar. Allow to stew gently until the fruit is cooked. Scatter the cornflour over the fruit mixture with a metal spoon and stir well together. Cook gently for a few minutes to allow the flour to blend in, then remove the saucepan from the heat and allow to cool.

Meanwhile, take the smaller pastry lid from the fridge and decorate with the pastry leaves by moistening their undersides with water and arranging in an attractive design. Brush over with milk. Fill the pastry flan case with the fruit mixture and put to bake near the top of a hot oven, 400°F (Gas 6), for 10 minutes, then reduce the heat to 375°F (Gas 5) for 20 minutes. Bake the pastry lid separately on a lower shelf until golden and cooked through.

Remove the flan from the oven when cooked and allow to cool. Push off the flan ring, place the pastry lid on top and serve hot or cold with thick fresh cream.

Rich Rice Pudding

In these days of convenience food and instant meals there are times when I long for a comforting, old-fashioned dish of rice pudding like our dear Lily Ogg used to cook for us in a battered oil stove at our family home at Castlepark, Huntly. I can see that pudding yet, with its dark caramelised skin which was all speckled with nutmeg and about a quarter of an inch thick. Under this was a layer of creamy custard and sultanas all plump and juicy and bursting with sweetness. This is the recipe.

2 oz. long grain rice
1½ oz. butter
2 large eggs
freshly grated nutmeg
1½ pints milk
3 oz. caster sugar
grated rind of half a lemon
small handful of sultanas

Put rice into a saucepan, pour the milk on and bring it slowly to simmering point and let it cook very gently until the rice is almost tender (about 10 minutes). Now stir in the sugar and the butter and stir until the sugar has dissolved and the butter has melted. Add the sultanas and stir again. Remove the saucepan from the heat and, when the mixture has cooled a little, stir in the beaten eggs and the lemon peel. Now turn the mixture into a well-buttered 2-pint pudding dish, sprinkle the surface with some freshly grated nutmeg, and bake the pudding in a pre-heated oven, 300°F (Gas 2), for about 40–45 minutes, by which time the rice will be cooked with a creamy layer of custard on top.

Flummery Drambuie

In the experimental kitchen at our factory on Speyside we have a fine team of food specialists including two chefs, David Sharp and Hugh Stephen. This recipe for flummery drambuie is one of David's favourites and he often makes it for overseas customers when they are visiting us. It is light and delicate in texture and rounds off a meal to perfection.

2 egg yolks
½ egg shell of sugar
1 measure Drambuie

½ egg shell of cold water
2 oz. lightly whipped cream

Place the eggs, water and sugar in double boiler. Beat and cook eggs over low heat until 'ribbon' stage is reached. The eggs should be very pale in colour and the consistency where the whisk leaves a trail. Allow the eggs to cool slightly, add the Drambuie, replace on heat and take back to 'ribbon' stage. Allow to cool, then carefully add the cream, folding gently. Serve with Savoy biscuits.

Orange and Lemon Flan

Orange and lemon flan is the choice of Hugh Stephen and this is his recipe.

8 oz. packet Rich Tea or Digestive biscuits
2 oz. butter
1 oz. raisins
1 oz. walnuts
1 oz. sugar
2 fresh lemons
1 fresh orange
1 large tin condensed milk
2 oz. fresh cream

Crush biscuits, chop walnuts and mix in raisins. Melt butter and sugar and add to biscuit mixture. Press mixture firmly into an 8-inch flan tin and chill until set. Grate rind from half lemon and half orange. Extract juice from one and a half lemons and half an orange. Reserve remainder of fruit for decoration. Add juice and rinds to the condensed milk, stirring slowly until mixture becomes thick. Leave to set, and decorate with remaining whipped piped cream and fruit.

Rothesay, Bute

Rothesay Pudding

- *2 oz. margarine*
- *2 tablespoons raspberry or strawberry jam*
- *1 level teaspoon baking soda*
- *1 teacup self-raising flour*
- *1 teacup breadcrumbs*
- *1 teacup milk*

Rub the margarine into the flour, then mix in the breadcrumbs, jam and soda, dissolved in the warm milk. Steam in a greased and covered basin for 1½–2 hours. Turn out and serve with custard or jam sauce.

Raspberries with Banana Sauce

Moray is favoured with a pleasant climate, seldom too cold in winter or too hot in summer. This coastal plain, with its rich alluvial soil, is tucked between the Cairngorm mountains and the sea. A fine farming area, it is well suited to soft fruit growing and my brother-in-law, Ian, farms many acres of strawberries and raspberries which eventually find their way into cans and jars in our food factory at Fochabers. In summer we have fresh fruit for dessert every day. I have made them into soufflés, pies and tarts, but the family still enjoy them fresh with cream and with banana sauce.

Banana Sauce

Mash three bananas with the juice of half a lemon until they are smooth. Stir in $\frac{1}{2}$ pint of double cream and 3 tablespoons icing sugar. Beat until the mixture is creamy. Serve the fresh raspberries from a bowl and hand round the banana sauce separately.

Strawberries Beaujolais

This is another delicious recipe I make in summer.

Prepare the fruit and put into a glass serving bowl. Boil $\frac{1}{4}$ lb. sugar and $\frac{1}{4}$ pint of water together until they form a syrup. Skim if necessary. Allow to cool, then add 1 glass of Beaujolais and 1 tablespoon brandy and pour the mixture over the strawberries. Stand in a cool place for several hours. Serve with whipped cream sweetened with icing sugar folded through it.

Finally, to end the desserts, I would like to give the recipes for two of the most successful sweets I have ever made. They are excellent for dinner parties.

Glenfiddich Chocolate Mousse

6 oz. sweet chocolate
1 teaspoon vanilla extract
$\frac{1}{2}$ pint double cream
5 eggs, separated
1 teaspoon instant coffee
2 tablespoons Glenfiddich (or any good whisky)

Melt the chocolate in a double boiler over simmering hot water. Remove from the heat and allow to cool. Lightly beat the egg yolks and stir them gradually into the melted chocolate. Flavour to taste with vanilla and instant coffee diluted in a tablespoon of hot water. Beat the cream until thick, stir in the whisky and fold into the chocolate mixture. Beat the egg whites until stiff and fold into the mixture a little at a time. Pour into a serving dish and chill for at least 2 hours.

Apple Amber Pudding

1½ lb. dessert apples (Cox's Pippins are best), cored and
  sliced
2 tablespoons butter
2 egg yolks, beaten
2 egg whites
vanilla extract
2–3 tablespoons sugar
grated rind of 1 lemon
8 oz. shortcrust pastry
1 tablespoon caster sugar
glacé cherries
angelica

Combine apples, sugar, butter and grated lemon rind in a saucepan and simmer gently, stirring from time to time until the mixture is reduced to a pulp. Beat the mixture until smooth, then add beaten egg yolks. Line a pie dish with pastry and pour in apple mixture. Bake in a moderate oven (375°F; Gas 4) for 30–40 minutes, until the pastry is cooked and the apple mixture set. Whisk egg whites until stiff, flavour with one tablespoon caster sugar and a few drops of vanilla. Pile meringue on top of the pudding, decorate with glacé cherries and angelica. Return to cool oven until lightly browned.

This pudding is also very good cold.

Baking

Scotland is often known as 'Land o' Cakes' and Scottish housewives must be the best bakers in the world. Oatcakes, scones in infinite variety (girdle, oven, fruit, soda, afternoon tea), pancakes, Dundee cakes, gingerbread, shortbread—the list is endless. I have often wondered why this is so. It may be because of our climate—where a cup of tea and a 'piece' is often made to cheer us up or heat us up when we arrive home on a cold day, or it may be due to the fact that Scotland is a small country made up of towns rather than big cities and therefore in small communities we all know each other and are consequently visiting and being entertained to tea and coffee.

Perhaps the main reason is our tradition of high tea, where the family sit down at six o'clock to a meal of fish or bacon and eggs, accompanied by bread, butter and jam, scones and cakes. There is a lot to be said for high tea. Once it is over the family have the rest of the evening free to indulge in their chosen pastime.

Ayrshire Shortbread

4 oz. rice flour
4 oz. caster sugar
2 tablespoons thin cream
4 oz. plain flour
½ beaten egg
4 oz. butter

Sieve the flours into a mixing bowl and rub in the butter with the fingers. Mix in the sugar and bind the mixture to a stiff consistency with the egg and cream. Roll out thinly, prick with a fork and cut into rounds or fingers. Place the shortbread on a greased paper on a greased baking sheet and bake in a steady oven for 15 minutes until pale golden in colour. Cool on a wire tray, dust with sugar and allow to get cold before using.

Petticoat Tails

1 lb. flour
8 oz. butter
6 oz. caster sugar
water or milk, as required

Sift the flour into a basin and rub in the butter. Stir in the sugar and enough milk or water to make a smooth

The Ayrshire coast at Girvan

dough. Divide into equal portions. Roll each rather
thinly into two rounds about the size of a dinner plate.
Crimp the edges and cut a round from the centre of each
with a cutter about 4 inches in diameter or cut round a
saucer inverted on top. Keep this inner circle whole and
cut the outer one into eight 'petticoat tails' or triangles.
Slip the rounds and the tails on to a lightly greased
baking sheet covered with greaseproof paper, keeping
them slightly apart. Bake at a temperature of 350°F (Gas
4) for about 20 minutes. Cool on a wire rack and dust
with caster sugar.

Shortbread Fingers

4 oz. plain flour
2 oz. rice flour
4 oz. butter
2 oz. caster sugar

Sieve the flour and the rice flour, then add the sugar and
butter. Work all together with the hands until the
consistency of shortcrust pastry. Form into a square
cake and cut into fingers. Pinch the edges and prick all
over with a fork. Bake in a steady oven (325°F, Gas 3)
until beginning to colour, then lower the heat and crisp
off slowly for about 1 hour. Cool on a wire tray.

Pancakes

3 heaped tablespoons self-raising flour
¼ teaspoon bicarbonate of soda
1 tablespoon caster sugar
¼ teaspoon salt
¼ teaspoon cream of tartar
1 egg
milk to mix

Clootie Dumpling

Tipsy Laird

Traditional Breakfast showing Porridge, Kippers, Aberdeen Buttery Rowies & Oatmeal Baps

Typical High Tea showing Smoked Haddock Scramble, Fochabers Gingerbread, White Girdle Scones, Shortbread & Pancakes

Heat a girdle or large frying pan. Sieve the dry ingredients and add the sugar. Drop in the whole egg and gradually beat to a thick cream with milk. Lightly grease the surface of the girdle or frying pan. Drop spoonfuls of the mixture on to the hot surface. When bubbles appear turn and cook for a further minute or so. Place between a folded cloth. Repeat the process until the batter is finished.

Fochabers Gingerbread

8 oz. butter
8 oz. sugar
8 oz. treacle
2 eggs
½ pint of beer
1 lb. flour
4 oz. sultanas
4 oz. currants
3 oz. ground almonds
3 oz. finely chopped candied peel
2 level teaspoons mixed spices
4 level teaspoons ground ginger
2 level teaspoons ground cinnamon
1 level teaspoon ground cloves
1 teaspoon bicarbonate of soda

Beat together the butter and sugar to a cream. Warm the treacle slightly and add. Then break in the eggs one at a time, beating well. Mix together the flour, fruit and ground almonds and the spices. Add to the butter mixture. Dissolve the bicarbonate of soda in the beer and add to the mixture. Mix together thoroughly. Put into buttered cake tins and bake in the centre of a slow oven (300°F, Gas 3) for about 2 hours. Remove from the tins and cool. Store in a tightly covered tin.

Pitcaithly Bannock

  6 oz. flour
  1 oz. rice flour
  4 oz. butter
  3 oz. caster sugar
  1 oz. almonds
  1 oz. mixed peel

Blanch the almonds, removing skins, and chop finely. Finely shred and chop peel. Mix the flour, rice flour and sugar in a mixing bowl; add the butter and work in all the ingredients, including the almonds and the peel. Roll out into a round flat cake about ¾ inch thick, pinch the edge with finger and thumb. Lay on a greased and papered tray and bake in a moderate oven (350°F, Gas 4) for 30–35 minutes.

White Girdle Scones

  1 lb. flour
  1 teaspoon cream of tartar
  1 teaspoon bicarbonate of soda
  ½ teaspoon salt
  a jug of milk

Sieve the dry ingredients into a mixing bowl. Add enough milk (the old Scottish housewife would probably have used sour milk) to make a soft, pliable dough. Turn out on to a floured board and divide into four. Knead each piece into a round scone with the hands to about ½ inch in thickness. Cut each into quarters, flour them and place on a hot, greased girdle or hot plate. Let them cook steadily until well risen and light brown underneath, then turn with a flat spatula and cook on the other side for about five minutes until the edges are dry. Fold in a clean tea towel and eat with butter and jam. These scones are best eaten fresh as they do not store well.

Treacle Scones

8 oz. flour
½ level teaspoon bicarbonate of soda
1 tablespoon caster sugar
½ tablespoon ground ginger
pinch of salt
½ oz. butter
1 tablespoon melted treacle
milk

Sieve the dry ingredients into a mixing bowl. Rub in the butter with the fingertips, then stir in the treacle. Add enough milk to make a softish dough. Roll out into a round on a floured board. Cut into rounds, and bake on a greased baking sheet in a hot oven (425°F, Gas 7) for 10–12 minutes.

Oatmeal Raisin Puffs

8 oz. raisins
½ cup sugar
a little water
1 cup fine oatmeal
¼ teaspoon baking soda
1 cup self-raising flour
pinch salt
½ teaspoon cinnamon
4 oz. margarine
milk

Put the raisins and the sugar into a saucepan with a little water and simmer slowly until the fruit is tender. Leave to cool. Sieve the flour, salt and cinnamon into a bowl. Add the oatmeal and rub in the margarine until the mixture resembles breadcrumbs. Dissolve the baking soda in enough milk to bind to a paste. Roll out and cut into rounds. Put a spoonful of raisins on half the rounds and cover with remaining rounds. Press edges and bake in a fairly hot oven for 20–30 minutes.

Barley Bannocks

> 1 teacup barley meal
> 1 level teaspoon salt
> 1 rounded teaspoon cream of tartar
> 1 teacup flour
> 1 level teaspoon baking soda
> about 1 teacup of milk

Mix dry ingredients, stir in enough milk to make a fairly soft mixture. Divide mixture into three or four pieces, knead and roll out each about half an inch thick. Place on a hot girdle and bake for a minute or two, till brown on the under side. Turn and bake on the outside, opening up the edge a little to see if bannock is cooked through.

Soda Bread

> 1 lb. flour
> 1 rounded teaspoon baking soda
> 1 oz. margarine
> 1 rounded teaspoon salt
> 2 rounded teaspoons cream of tartar
> about ½ pint milk

Sieve the dry ingredients into a basin, then rub in the margarine and stir in enough milk to make a soft dough. Knead quickly and lightly, form into two round loaves, place on a floured baking tray and bake in a hot oven (400°F, Gas 6) for about 30 minutes till well risen, lightly browned and firm in the centre.

Sultana Malt Loaf

8 oz. self-raising flour
good pinch of salt
3 oz. sultanas
1 teaspoon baking soda
1½ tablespoons syrup
1½ tablespoons malt extract
a little milk

Mix dry ingredients in a basin. Melt syrup and malt in a pan and stir into dry ingredients along with beaten egg, and milk if necessary, to make a softish dough. Turn into a greased loaf tin, brush over with milk and bake in a moderate oven for 45 minutes to 1 hour, till well risen, firm and brown.

Abernethy Biscuits

8 oz. flour
3 oz. margarine or lard and margarine mixed
2 rounded tablespoons fine sugar
1 level teaspoon baking powder
pinch of salt
1 egg, beaten
a little milk

Mix flour, baking powder, rub in fat, then add the sugar. Mix in enough egg and milk to make a stiff paste. Knead on a lightly floured board, roll out to ¼ inch thick. Cut into rounds and prick all over with a fork. Bake on a greased tray in a moderate oven for 10 to 15 minutes or till pale brown. Cool on a wire tray.

Girdle Parkins

2 tablespoons sugar
1 level dessert spoon margarine
1½ teacups fine oatmeal

1 *egg, beaten*
2 *tablespoons treacle*
1 *teacup flour*
1 *level teaspoon cinnamon and ginger mixed*
a little milk

Melt margarine, sugar and treacle. Mix dry ingredients, then stir in the melted mixture, along with the beaten egg, adding milk if required to make a thick, dropping consistency. Drop portions from a tablespoon on to a moderately hot girdle. Bake until firm and lightly browned underneath, then turn to finish on the other side. Cool on a wire tray. If these are baked in the oven, allow about 20 minutes at a moderate heat.

Oatmeal Bap

1 *breakfast cup oatmeal*
1 *breakfast cup flour*
1 *breakfast cup sour milk*
1 *rounded teaspoon salt*
1 *rounded teaspoon baking soda*

Soak the oatmeal in the milk overnight. Sift flour, salt and soda together, and stir into the soaked oatmeal, adding more flour if necessary, to make a fairly stiff mixture. Knead and roll to a round about 2 inches thick. Place on a floured tray, mark into sections, and bake in a fairly hot oven for 20 minutes or longer, till cooked through and lightly browned.

Banffshire Tea Biscuits

4 *level teaspoons baking powder*
1 *level teaspoon salt*
1 *cup milk*
2 *cups flour*
3 *level teaspoons lard*

Sift together the baking powder, flour and salt. Rub in the lard until the consistency of shortcrust pastry. Add the milk and mix lightly and quickly. Toss the dough on to a floured board and knead 3 or 4 times very lightly. Bake in a hot oven, 12–15 minutes.

Highland Biscuits

2 teacups flour
4 oz. margarine
1 teaspoon water
$\frac{1}{2}$ lb. brown sugar
1 egg yolk

Sift the flour and mix in the sugar. Rub in fat and knead to a dough. Roll out and cut into rounds. Mix 1 teaspoon water with egg yolk and brush over the biscuits. Bake in a moderate oven (375°F, Gas 5) for 30 minutes.

Fruit Squares

8 oz. shortcrust pastry
1 small apple
2 tablespoons sugar
12 oz. seedless raisins
$\frac{1}{4}$ teaspoonful cinnamon

Roll out pastry and cut into two. Line a greased swiss roll tin with half the pastry. Cook the raisins, sugar, apple and cinnamon in a little water for about five minutes. Cool, then place over pastry. Roll out the remainder of the pastry and cover the fruit, pressing the edges down with a fork. Bake in a moderate oven (375°F, Gas 5) until slightly brown. Remove and sprinkle with caster sugar. Cut in squares when cold.

Dunlop Cheese Loaf

8 oz. self-raising flour
½ level teaspoon dry mustard
pinch cayenne pepper
½ level teaspoon onion or celery salt
2 oz. butter or margarine
4 oz. finely grated Dunlop cheddar
1 beaten egg made up to ¼ pint with milk

Lightly grease a 2 lb. loaf tin. Sift the flour, mustard, cayenne pepper, onion or celery salt into a bowl. Add the butter or margarine and rub in to resemble fine breadcrumbs. Stir in grated cheese. Mix to a firm dough with the beaten egg and milk, using a knife. Turn on to a lightly floured board and knead gently till smooth. Form the dough into a roll the length of the prepared tin. Place in the tin and push out to fit evenly. Bake above centre in a moderate oven (375°F, Gas 5) for 35–45 minutes till golden, and the loaf sounds hollow when tapped on the base. Cool on a wire tray. Serve cut into slices and buttered well. Best eaten on the day it is made as it doesn't keep well.

Sweet Bannocks

7 oz. fine oatmeal
4 oz. self-raising flour
4 oz. sugar
2 oz. lard
1 oz. margarine
4 tablespoons water

Mix oatmeal, flour and sugar in a bowl. Melt the lard and margarine with water in a saucepan and pour into the bowl. Mix well and turn on to a floured board. Roll out and cut with scone cutter. Bake for 15 minutes at 400°F (Gas 6). Turn off the oven and leave for a further 15 minutes. Delicious with marmalade for breakfast or with jam for tea.

Raisin Shortbread

4 oz. butter
4–6 oz. seedless raisins
2 oz. caster sugar
6 oz. plain flour
4–6 tablespoons orange squash

Put the orange squash and seedless raisins in a small saucepan and bring slowly to the boil. Turn into a basin and leave to cool. Sieve the flour and sugar into a mixing bowl and rub in the butter. Knead into a dough, divide in two and form into two equal sized squares. Place one square on a greased baking sheet, spread the raisins on top and cover with the second square. Press down firmly, pinch the edges and prick well. Bake at 350°F (Gas 4) for 45 minutes. Mark into squares and when cool remove from the tin.

Old-fashioned Ginger Parkin

4 oz. plain flour
½ teaspoon cinnamon
¾ teaspoon bicarbonate of soda
8 oz. fine or medium oatmeal
1 heaped teaspoon ground ginger
8 oz. black treacle
8 oz. soft brown sugar
3 oz. butter or margarine
1 egg
5–6 tablespoons milk

Sieve together flour, cinnamon, ginger and bicarbonate of soda. Add oatmeal to dry ingredients. Slowly melt butter, treacle and sugar in saucepan and add with beaten egg to the flour mixture. Stir in milk and mix thoroughly to form a fairly soft batter. Turn into a prepared greaseproof-paper-lined shallow tin about 1¼ inches deep. Bake in a moderate oven (350°F, Gas 4) for 25 minutes and then at 325°F (Gas 3), for 20–30 minutes. Cut the next day into thick squares.

Moist Fruit Ginger Cake

6 oz. butter or margarine
6 oz. sugar
2 beaten eggs
10 oz. plain flour
½ teaspoon bicarbonate of soda
½ teaspoon cinnamon
3 oz. walnuts
6 oz. sultanas
2 oz. syrup
2 oz. treacle
2 teaspoons ground ginger
milk if required

Cream the butter or margarine and the sugar and gradually beat in the eggs. Mix well. Work in the flour and add the other ingredients. If necessary add a little milk to make a moist, but not wet, consistency. Bake in a prepared cake tin in a moderate oven (350°F, Gas 4) for about 2 hours.

Eyemouth Tart

2 oz. walnuts
2 oz. currants
2 oz. coconut
2 oz. cherries
1 oz. butter (melted)
2 oz. raisins
3 oz. sugar
1 egg (beaten)
8 oz. icing sugar
8 oz. shortcrust pastry

Roll out pastry and use to line a swiss roll tin. Mix the dry ingredients, add beaten egg and melted butter. Spread the mixture over the pastry and bake in the oven (375°F, Gas 5) till golden brown. Mix the icing sugar with a very little cold water, and ice while still hot.

Nice and Easy Fruit Cake

This fruit cake was the first cake I ever tried to bake and it turned out very successfully. I still make it and send it to my son who is away at boarding school. It is just as popular and as nice and easy to make as ever.

6 oz. butter
6 oz. sugar
3 beaten eggs
1 rounded teaspoon baking powder
9 oz. plain flour
8 oz. dried mixed fruit
milk

Beat the butter and sugar to a cream, then beat in the flour and eggs thoroughly. Stir in the fruit and the baking powder and add a very little milk to make a dropping consistency. Turn into a greased tin (no need to line with greased paper) and bake for 2 hours. For the first half hour in a good moderate oven (350°F, Gas 4) then bake for $1\frac{1}{2}$ hours at a reduced heat (300°F, Gas 2).

Macduff Christmas Cake

1 lb. currants
1 lb. sultanas
4 oz. glacé cherries
4 oz. mixed peel
8 oz. ground almonds

8 oz. butter
8 oz. soft brown sugar
5 eggs
3 dessertspoons sherry
1 tablespoon treacle
10 oz. plain flour
1 teaspoon mixed spice
½ teaspoon ground cinnamon
½ teaspoon ground ginger
¼ teaspoon ground cloves
¼ teaspoon ground mace
¼ teaspoon ground nutmeg

Cream the butter and sugar. Add the eggs whole, one at a time, and beat in the treacle. Add the flour sieved with the spices, then the dried fruits, cherries, peel and ground almonds; lastly pour in the sherry. Cook in a pre-heated oven (350°F, Gas 4) for 30 minutes, then turn down the heat to 325°F, Gas 3 and bake for about another 2½ hours. Line cake tin with double greaseproof paper.

Whisky Cake

6 oz. sultanas
½ pint water
4 oz. butter
5 oz. caster sugar
1 egg
2 tablespoons whisky
6 oz. plain flour
1 level teaspoon bicarbonate of soda
¼ teaspoon salt
½ teaspoon grated nutmeg
1 tablespoon lemon juice
2½ oz. finely chopped walnuts

Cover sultanas with water and simmer for $\frac{1}{4}$ hour. Drain, but save a little of the liquid. Cream butter and sugar and beat in the egg. Stir in flour, bicarbonate of soda, salt and nutmeg alternately, with approximately 2 tablespoons of liquid from the sultanas. Stir in sultanas, lemon juice, chopped walnuts and whisky. Pour into two 8-inch sandwich tins and bake for 30 minutes at 350°F (Gas 4).

Filling and Topping

- 2 oz. butter
- 7 oz. icing sugar
- 2 tablespoons lemon juice
- 1 dessertspoon whisky

Cream butter and sugar until smooth. Add the lemon juice and the whisky and beat further until the consistency of smooth cream. Use half to sandwich the two cakes together and the remainder put into an icing bag with a star nozzle and pipe a trellis design across the top.

Note: this cake is not suitable for storing.

Table of Measures

My husband Gordon and I have visited the U.S.A. and Canada on business many times and have enjoyed great hospitality from these warm-hearted and friendly people. Their cookery measures differ slightly from ours, but it is quite easy to make the necessary conversions.

For our many American and Canadian friends, here they are.

Solids

BRITISH MEASURE		AMERICAN MEASURE
Flour: $\frac{1}{4}$ lb. or 4 oz.	=	1 standard cup
Sugar: 6 oz.	=	1 standard cup
Breadcrumbs: 2 oz.	=	1 standard cup
Raisins: 6 oz.	=	1 standard cup
Rice: $\frac{1}{2}$ lb. or 8 oz.	=	1 standard cup
Chopped meat (packed): $\frac{1}{2}$ lb. or 8 oz.	=	1 standard cup
Butter and fat: $\frac{1}{2}$ lb. or 8 oz.	=	1 standard cup
Flour: 1 oz.	=	4 level standard tablespoons
Sugar: 1 oz.	=	2 level standard tablespoons
Syrup or treacle: 1 oz.	=	2 level standard tablespoons
Butter: 1 oz.	=	2 level standard tablespoons

Liquids

1 pint	=	$2\frac{2}{3}$ standard cups
$\frac{1}{2}$ pint	=	$1\frac{1}{3}$ standard cups
$\frac{1}{4}$ pint	=	$\frac{2}{3}$ standard cups

In the recipes where cups and spoons are used these refer to *British* handy measures, but can easily be converted to *American* standard measures.

BRITISH		AMERICAN
1 average teacup	=	approximately 1 American standard cup
1 average rounded tablespoon	=	approximately 2 level American standard tablespoons
1 rounded teaspoon (baking powder etc.)	=	2 level American standard teaspoons

When measuring dry ingredients, make sure that all cups and spoonfuls are level.

Index